ISSUES

of

MANHOOD

in

BLACK *AND* WHITE

ISSUES
of
MANHOOD
in
BLACK AND WHITE

*An Incisive Look into Masculinity and
the Societal Definition of Afrikan Man*

Amos N. Wilson

Afrikan World InfoSystems
New York

FIRST EDITION 2017
ISBN 10 : 1-879164-14-0
ISBN 13 : 978-1-879164-14-7

Part II of this publication, *Understanding Black Adolescent Male Violence*,
was first published as ISBN 1-879164-03-5

Typographer and Executive Editor: SABABU N. PLATA
Assistant Editor: Adisa Makalani
Cover Illustrator: Joseph Gillians

Library of Congress Cataloging-in-Publication Data

Names: Wilson, Amos N., author.
Title: Issues of manhood in black and white : an incisive look into
masculinity and the societal definition of afrikan man / Amos N. Wilson.
Description: First Edition. | New York : Afrikan World InfoSystems, [2016] |
Includes bibliographical references and index.
Identifiers: LCCN 2016052103 | ISBN 1879164140 (pbk. : alk. paper)
Subjects: LCSH: Men--South Africa. | Masculinity--South Africa. |
Afrikaners--Social conditions.
Classification: LCC HQ1090.7.S6 W55 2016 | DDC 305.310968--dc23
LC record available at https://lccn.loc.gov/2016052103

Publisher:
AFRIKAN WORLD INFOSYSTEMS
743 Rogers Avenue, Suite 6/3L
Brooklyn, New York 11226
Email: Afrikanworld@aol.com

Printed in Canada
10 9 8 7 6 5 4 3 2 1

Dedicated

To Ahmes, and the young grappling
with the challenges of life

Editor's Note:

The conceptualization of this book came about in the 1990s but finally bore fruit (*be it bitter*) today amidst the cries of violence, police murder and brutality, unemployment, miseducation, housing displacement and the many forms of discrimination and ills that plague black society in the U.S. and the wider Diaspora. The relevance of this work has withstood the transit of time where topics die and are ultimately forgotten, only to rear their heads as new issues to an unknowing new generation. This chagrin thus makes our case.

When Dr. Wilson delivered this presentation in 1990, we were awaiting the large shipment of the newly completed *Black-on-Black Violence.* That afternoon, under the auspices of Afrikan Echoes, a communiversity group in Newark, New Jersey, Amos delivered a sterling presentation on Black manhood. Siting in the audience, I was bowled over by the brilliance of this erudition and always wished this to be in print for a larger, and future, audience. Later Amos wrote a small text *Understanding Black Adolescent Male Violence*, a well received piece, to partner *Black-on-Black Violence*, geared to addressing the youth arm of our movement then confronted by the crack cocaine epidemic. As with so many things, these ideas were tabled in place of other priorities, not to mention the passing of Dr. Wilson in 1995. Finally, in 2014, after reediting and re-engineering our books to meet the standards demanded by evolving technology, we resurrected this project, marrying the thoughts expressed then, with the modest *Understanding Black Adolescent Male Violence*. Here, we have since appropriately re-titled this November 1990 lecture, *Manhood in the Afrikan Diaspora: A Wringing Anthropological Retrospective on Male Obligation to Family, Community, and Nation*. Furthermore, we have at long last reunited these pieces in a two-for-one volume called *Issues of Manhood in Black and White: An Incisive Look into Masculinity and the Societal Definition of Afrikan Man*, one that expresses concern for the manufacture of positive males geared to undertake the challenges of a world angled towards their negation and/or possible destruction. The prescient thoughts expressed then, read as if written today.

CONTENTS

Part I

Manhood in the Afrikan Diaspora
A Wringing Anthropological Retrospective on
Male Obligation to Family, Community, and Nation

Part II

Understanding Black
Adolescent Male Violence
Its Prevention and Remediation

Part One

MANHOOD IN THE AFRIKAN DIASPORA

*A Wringing Anthropological
Retrospective on Male Obligation
to Family, Community, and Nation*

*Our ancestors watch and await
their return through our young*

Overview

Thank you very much for your warm reception and it's great to be among you again. I always enjoy appearing here, being with you, and sharing the time with you. Certainly, I'm happy to get your invitation. I'm going to talk a bit today about Afrikan manhood in the Diaspora, even though I see on your announcement the lecture was tentatively titled "Black-on-Black Violence." That's okay.

We had expected by this time to have my new publication, *Black-on-Black Violence*, and we had anticipated talking about it today. As you can see here, it's *Black-on-Black Violence: The Psychodynamics of Black Self-Annihilation in Service of White Domination*. We're waiting on the books to be delivered. Hopefully, they will be delivered tomorrow or by Tuesday and they will be in your local store before the end of the week. We hope you'll be able to pick them up and sort of let us know what you think about the book.

As you can see though, we're concerned with black-on-black violence, but concerned with it in terms of the political context in which it occurs, as you can tell from the subtitle. We see black-on-black violence as a form of black self-annihilation in service to white domination. We have to look beyond the mere idea that so-called criminality and violence in the black community is the result of crack cocaine. People are motivated to take and smoke crack, engage in the selling of it and into all of the activities so related. Of course, there was violence in our community prior to the crack epidemic, so we cannot blame that violence merely on the existence of crack.

We must, though, recognize that criminal behavior, black-on-black violence, represents a form of social relationship. It isn't often we think of criminal behavior as a social relationship, but it is. A person in fact chooses to relate to another person in a particular sort of way, in a way that leads to

1

violence being committed against one or both of those individuals. That commitment of violence and that social interaction is a result of social attitudes, prior learning, miseducation and other social and political factors. So in order to understand what motivates black-on-black violence, we have to understand the social system in which that violence occurs. If we are talking about our children mugging other children for sneakers or for jackets and so forth, we must recognize that the fact that they are mugging and hurting each other for those jackets, sneakers and so forth must occur within a social system where these things are produced and valued. So, in effect, the crime is still a social, political, economic product. Consequently, we have to study the economics of criminality.

The general system would make us think that criminal behavior — black-on-black violence, or violence in general — is the result of some criminal tendency in the individual; that somehow the criminal is greatly different from the rest of the people in the population; that there is some type of twisted values. We try to illustrate in this particular text how those things that motivate black-on-black violence and criminality are continuous with standard everyday values. As a matter of fact, the black-on-black violent criminal is very much what I call a bourgeois criminal. The things he's attacking people for are the same things that the "good old" black middle class struggles so hard for, not different. They are different only in technique and approach. But it indicates there's a sharing of values between what we call our black-on-black criminals and what we call our normal law-abiding people. As a matter of fact, I will try demonstrating here that it is the very law-abidingness of black people that sets this thing up. It is our failure to come to terms with what law is, where it comes from, why laws are instituted, how laws themselves are the major contributors to criminality and are a major part of the problem. So in order to begin to change this situation that confronts us today with the murder of our children on the streets and so forth and the destruction of our communities, we have to upgrade our understanding of the motivations that moves our people to attack and destroy one another.

This book is in line with the other books I have written *(The Developmental Psychology of the Black Child)*, with the one I hope to have published around February, the working title being *On the Education of Black Children*, where I do an extensive analysis of some of the issues dealing with the education of our children, how our children are set-up through the kind of educational system we have today (which is really not an educational system, but a *mis*-education system) and how we must come to terms and begin at the beginning — that we are operating in an oppressive system.

That sounds like old hat to a lot of us. Many of us want to say, "Wow, that's 60s talk; we've heard it before." We really have *not* heard it before, in order for us to be in the condition we're in as people. There is hearing and there is listening. A lot of us have heard it, perhaps, but a lot of us have not listened. I talk about listening in the sense that after hearing, one moved forward. But if we're still talking about the things we were talking about in the 60s, it's because somewhere we are not listening to what is going on. Often we take superficial sameness to mean that sameness in terms of depth.

We must again look at this oppressive situation. Often when I go to conferences, educational and so forth, I see people diving directly into the discussion of the education of our children *without* discussing the context in which that education takes place. You are going to waste tremendous amounts of time and destroy your children if you don't look at the context in which a phenomenon occurs. This happens all too often. Some of you may have heard me a few weeks ago on the Lloyd Strayhorn show when we started to talk about why our children have problems in mathematics. I'll next appear on that show on the third of December. I made the generalization that our children have problems in mathematics because they *must* have problems in mathematics.[1]

It's not merely a matter of whether they're able to learn math, have the motivation and all the things we are talking about. You have to look at what would the learning of mathematics means to European domination; what would the learning of technological thinking mean to the hegemony of the white man on this earth today; what would the establishment of black research libraries, the entry of Afrikan nations into the space race *for real*, the manufacture by Afrikan people of technological systems and so forth mean economically, politically, and militarily to Europeans? You have to start with that first. If you don't start with that you miss the whole point of the deal.

If, then, our technological expertise, abundance and so forth is a threat to European dominance, then it should not come as a surprise to you that in a school designed by Europeans for Europeans, black children would have their largest numbers of problems around the technological areas. It is there where you start, before you get into the motivational systems of the students. You will recognize that once that system sees our technological advancement as *inimical* to their dominance, they are going to organize the motivational system of the youth so it would appear they voluntarily avoid mathematics, science, and technological thinking. They are going to organize that motivational system so almost in no way will you be able to teach mathematics in the deep sense. You can concentrate on one technique after another and you'll end with the same problem. This is the reason why people are so frustrated today. Every year there's a new technique, a new approach that's going to *magically* get our children to read and write. Of course you find yourself the next year asking, "What happened to this program that had such great promise?"

You start there and work that through in depth. And it's not enough just to say, "They want us to fail because it keeps them in power." That's the first statement. Then, of course, you've got to go into *how* the failure is created — psychologically, socially, economically, politically and so forth — and get into the fine points of the organization of the Afrikan psyche such that it maintains European dominance. After you work that out, then you get into what is *our* definition of education. Too many of us enter into this discussion not having defined our basic terms, using the words of Europeans. Those words have a history to them.[2]

Power of Words

Words are not mere means of communications. Words have histories. Words represent political experiences. Words represent political, military and economic intentions. Words are the organizers of thinking and behavior; they're not mere means of sharing ideas, not by a long shot. Words are the means by which people manipulate each other's consciousness and through the manipulation of their consciousness their behavior, their vision, their perception and the way they relate one to the other. That's why you have to have a very sound knowledge of words. Some people who have reviewed this book have already talked to me about the words in the book. Well, you're going to have to wrestle with it a little bit, but that's all right. We've got to wrestle with words. We are victimized by an absence of knowledge of words and word power. We've got to move beyond the linguistic level in which we operate now as people. A great part of the oppression of our people occurs at the point of word usage. We have to be able to recognize how language is used so that we'll learn how to use it as a tool and weapon against those who would dominate us as such. Later on I hope to do a book about the health of our people from the psychosomatic point of view; again, a further extension of this topic. Black-on-black violence is bad for our health obviously and in a sense it is a part of our killing ourselves for white-folk. When you let a people dominate you mentally, spiritually and psychologically, they implant a spirit in you. And, of course, they implant that spirit so that spirit can take over your body, your desires, your behaviors and perceptions to carry out their wishes.

In this book I talk about desire. You have to recognize that the whole white system is founded on Afrikan desire. I want you to look at that because I think it's very important. If we didn't desire certain things, the system could not last. But when we can't live without every piece of garbage and junk those people offer us, then we maintain the very system. I give an example about the taking of crack and how the whole crack establishment is based on desire — the desire of the addict. You remove that desire for crack and you've removed the whole institutional set-up, the whole arrangement. Gone. I talked about how that desire in the crack addict is not only a personal desire but really a form of organization of the total community. Do you see what the desire for crack does to a community, how it reorganizes the total community structure, how it reorganizes the way people relate one to another? Look at how a family becomes reorganized based on a desire for crack? So a desire is not merely an individual thing; it's not merely a wish to fill a craving on the part of the individual. Not at all. We relate to other people in terms of our desires. Therefore, when you let other people manufacture for you — and in manufacturing, manufacture desires — they also manufacture the organization of your social relations and the whole system of relations you have one to the other. So we have to look at how we've come to desire.

Thus the demon, the spirit is implanted in us so that the things we desire are the very things that support the total system. That comes in the form of words, language and other things. This is the reason why we have to analyze those kinds of things when we talk about health in this regard. If whites have a death wish — and they do — toward black folk, and white folks fill the head of blacks with white-produced desires, concepts, words and so forth, then we as people will get sick and die for white folk. You can see us dying in many forms. Black-on-black violence is one of them; poor health habits is another, all kinds of psychosomatic diseases (high blood pressure, heart disease). Many of the other diseases we talk about today are a result of the fact that we are carrying out the white death-wish in our own personalities, even to the point of Saudi Arabia. Black health and so forth is supremely connected to the political structure.

You must begin to recognize that health is political. Many of us are so miseducated in this system until we think of disease as merely a biological phenomenon. Of course it's often taught in the school that way. "Cancer is caused by some kind of radiation, or this and that," we are told. But it is documented that those people who live closer to waste dumps and atomic plants tend to get it more frequently; therefore, a good way of reducing the disease is to move the people. However, the people are there because of political and power differences. So the disease is not only the result of a biological syndrome working its way through the body; it is often primarily a result of a political, economic syndrome working its way through the body politic. It is not enough for us to merely understand the biological mechanisms of disease; we must come to understand the political, social and economic mechanisms of disease.[3]

You can thus begin to see where an Afrikan-centered education is so, so different from what we're getting today. It's not just preparing for jobs and skills and that kind of nonsense; it's about life, surviving, overthrowing and being liberated as a people, because you can die *with* these skills. The accumulation by black people of mere knowledge, the accumulation by Afrikan people of mere skills, in no way provides protection for us as a people. It's not going to do it.

The young man here who made an announcement introduced a very important concept — a nation-within-a-nation. If you are not discussing a nation-within-a-nation, if you are not thinking of yourself as a people *separate and distinct* in this country and operate as such, you are wasting your time accumulating knowledge and information; you're going to *die* black and proud. It's not enough to become Afrocentric in your knowledge; it is not enough to collect skills. Skills and knowledge must be organized *under* the general purpose of the people themselves or else it doesn't matter.

The working of whites in this country (even though they may see going to their jobs as individual activities), the sum total of those individual activities represents the strength of this nation. They represent its capacity to militarily defend them against their enemy. Their going to work with their skills represents the power of this nation to dominate in the world. They may think that they're just going for their own personal reasons, but because they have a nation and their going to work is subsumed under national goals, their very jobs actually are created or phased in and out based on national policy. These jobs just don't occur simply because somebody happens to want to hire you. The very nation itself—through tax policies, political policies, subsidizing certain industries, through grants and other things—transforms occupational levels. You will see the state or the nation transforming occupations dependent upon what its enemies are doing.

Some of you were here when the Russians sent up the Sputnik. It frightened this country. Right away the Congress went into action and created the student defense loan program or whatever they called it. In other words, they put money into those people to go this way or that—to restructure. Those people, they went to college, they got jobs and maybe didn't even know the history of how those jobs came into being. But in following through—even in thinking in personal terms —they actually moved the nation forward and kept the nation powerful.

A group of Afrikan people who are merely qualified for jobs and have mere knowledge, but who do not operate within the context of a nation, are just a bunch of individuals who with all of their knowledge, experience and skills cannot defend themselves against their enemy and can be wiped out and destroyed. So education and so forth has to move far beyond the concept of mere accumulation of knowledge, or even beyond the concept of Afrikan history. It has got to be welded into peoplehood or else it is incomplete. And this is part of the thing we must work towards.

I'm going to talk a bit about *Afrikan manhood within the Diaspora,* an issue that I know bothers some people, particularly those feminists who have gotten their signs from the white feminists and who have let white feminism infiltrate their minds and have not examined it very closely. It has almost become unpopular to talk about what it means to be a man, to deal with the concept of manhood. You've got to deal with it. You can't get around it. Of course, I will mention that infamous book in a minute; it also deals with the concept of manhood.

Alarming Statistics

Let's look at a few headlines in relationship to our subject today. I'm looking at the *New York Times* piece of Sunday, September 30, 1990. Starting on the first page: "Milwaukee Creating 2 Schools for Black Boys." I'll just read a couple of quotes here.

> The school board has voted to create two African-American Immersion Schools in a pilot program that seeks to emphasize black culture, build self-esteem and promote the rewards of responsible male behavior.

You can see why people start hollering and screaming. Ladies and gentlemen, for us to be in the condition we are in, the black male must be perceived as irresponsible. Part of what I talk about in *Black-on-Black Violence* is what role do these men in jail serve in terms of maintaining European culture. Why are these aggressive men being put in these places? It has all to do with the definition of what it means to be a man. An oppressor recognizes it is far more likely that it is the male of the species who is going to resist domination — and resist it violently. Any oppressor who is worth his salt knows that you must destroy the males. You must imprison them, humiliate them and do any other kind of thing to them in order to hold a people down. A part of this so-called black-on-black violence is cued up with that. One of the reasons our men are in jail is not because of any criminality of the black man, but essentially the criminality of the white man. We must come to understand that. The thing I'm getting to here is that criminality and irresponsibility is centered around this concept of manhood.[4] It goes on to say:

> The Milwaukee plan, which was pushed by a group of black educators and parents, represents the most dramatic educational approach aimed at saving the next generation of young black men from the social maelstrom now devouring much of the current generation.

This talk of "next generation" reminds me of how they dragged out Kenneth Clark to rage impotently at what is going on. I wish the brother a very nice safe retirement. It's time; he's *earned* it! Yes, 36 years of the philosophy of Kenneth Clark. *Thirty-six years and what do we have to show for it?* Thirty-six years of assimilationism, integrationism, being taught by white folk and this other kind of stuff. Then you drag out the arch architect of that program to try to deal with this issue. What does he say here? "For adults to impose this nonsense on children is academic child abuse." What the heck does he think has been happening to black children since 1954? It's amazing. "It's outrageous, it's absurd! It's a continuation of the whole segregation nonsense," he continues.

Integration has theoretically little to do with education. We tried to warn you that the NAACP was not about the education of black children; it was about the integration of black children. And those two things are not co-terminous. Hopefully, we've learned our lesson and are seeing some reactions and changes to that.[5] Often, what is not talked about is the situation in Milwaukee. It says here:

> Educators are familiar with the consequences of the dire circumstances. Nearly one in four black American men in their 20's is in jail, on probation or parole, while 1 in 5 in that age group is in college.

I'm sure you're familiar with that statistic. One-fourth of our males are in jails, on parole, or in some relationship with the so-called criminal justice system.

> Among black males 18 to 34 years old, homicide is the leading cause of death [men killing each other in the interest of white domination]. . . . Fewer than 20 percent of black male students in Milwaukee schools maintain a C average or better.

This is part of the crux of the issue. What do you do when literally you have 80% of the males basically *flunking*, only 20% making a C-average or better, and the best thing our so-called leadership can do is to offer us more of the same old things that have not worked? These people are in a drastic set of circumstances (as we all are) and they recognize that some heavy changes had to be made if we're going to get out of it. It's too bad that we had to lose a generation or two of our people in order to learn this lesson when the knowledge, information and so forth was available to us right at that time. That means we have to change our way of learning. We cannot afford to take 20 and 36 years to learn basic lessons. This is one of the reasons why we have to learn to use the language. That's one of the reasons languages exist, so that the historical experience of a people can be passed onto the next generation without that generation having to go through the same experience that the prior generation went through. That's the essence of the teaching between grandmother and child, mother and child, teacher and student.

Words represent the accumulated experience of a people. Why then don't they want black children to read? So that the accumulated experience of black people and accumulated experience of knowledgeable people cannot be passed onto them; so that they'll make the same stumbling mistakes that have been made generation after generation after generation. That's why they have difficulty reading, ladies and gentlemen, so that they cannot *break* the codes of their enemies, see through those codes, learn rapidly and avoid the sacrifice of two and three and four generations of their people before they learn the lesson. That's why we have to know words; that's why we have to know the language.

The Kenneth Clark experiment itself had right in it the contradictions, but we were *so* caught up in our desire to be with white-folk, into thinking that it would solve all our problems. "You solve all your problems by running into the arms of your enemies." I can't understand it. Those people announce, "I don't want your children! I don't like your children!" "Take them anyhow," we plead. Just forcing them. It was an amazing situation we saw in the 1960s and 70s. Unbelievable. We expected that if we forced our children on them, they were going to educate them for us. "Now, what's wrong with our children?" You know what's wrong with your children.[6]

> Black boys accounted for 50 percent of all school suspensions here last year, although they represent less than 28 percent of the enrollment. Minority pupils made up more than 70percent of the district's enrollment.

It goes on with various other things about the education of males. Another quick citation here from the *Amsterdam News* on the 13th of October 1990, talking about the New York State correctional system, in a report put out by the Correctional Association of New York and the New York State Coalition for Criminal Justice:

> Key findings in the study conducted by the Correctional Association of New York and the New York State Coalition for Criminal Justice note that young African-American men are over 23 times more likely to be jailed than white men.

In the book, *Black-on Black Violence*, I talk about statistics. In fact I have in a chapter there called "Quantifying the Myth," the arrest statistics, number of people in jail and what that means. We deal with this because it has a psychological effect on people when they read statistics. They assume the number of arrests indicates the level of criminality present in a people; so the more people you have in jail or the more people arrested, the more criminal they must be in nature. Many of us are psyched out by that. That's a myth and we have to deal with that myth.[7]

The number of men in jail represents the number of men who have been *arrested*. That's all it represents. In the purest sense of the word, you can be in jail without having committed a crime. Simply because you are in jail doesn't mean that you've committed a crime. Because you're in prison doesn't mean that you've committed a crime or that you are a criminal in the deep sense. It's a fallacious jump in logic to assume merely because our men outnumber the other groups in prison they are also then more criminal. Of course that's what the system wants to make you think; that's why they run the statistics. It knows that most people, having gone through this American *mis*education system (and they know our minds because they've trained them) will automatically jump: "Waw, these black men must really be criminal; so many of them are in jail." So many are *arrested*. Why aren't there more white men in jails? "Well, they must be less criminal?" Is that right?

What have I told you all the time about being under oppression? Under oppression, things must be turned *backwards*. In order for this system to be ruled, it must be ruled in terms of lies and deceptions. You don't have a minority population, a 10% minority population (like Europeans), ruling the world on the basis of truth, justice, honesty, and the "all-American way." You don't have that. It has to be twisted around. In order for the oppressed to comply with that system, the oppressed, too, must be backwards, believe lies, take lies for truth and truth for lies. We must understand that fundamental fact *before* you get into all other thinking. So what do we have? The crooks and thieves outside, and the victims in jail. The victims are called crooks and thieves, and the ones outside are the law-abiding citizens.

This white man is the greatest crook, thief, killer and murderer the world has ever known. For you to think this white man in non-criminal and represents what it means to be law-abiding, you've got to be out of your mind. You've got to be crazy. There are a lot of us who think that, but you *have* to in order for this system to work. That's one of the reasons why you have to educate your own children so they won't fall victim to this kind of mythology and the American mythology of "science-tizing" nonsense by covering it with numbers.

Because we live in this kind of culture we tend to think that if something carries a course number, it is valid. Of course, psychology is famous for representing political theories behind statistics, and people getting so caught up in the mathematical operations, they think because the mathematics balances and checks out, what is being talked about also balances and checks out. "That's the 5% (or whatever you call it) level of competence." It's still a lie. That's one of the reasons why psychologists are probably one of the most miseducated of professionals, because a lot of that hocus-pocus goes on there. You spend time after time with mathematics and statistics again and again. Often you still have to point out to people, "Hey, the math can check out very well, but what about the idea behind the math?" They're not intrinsically related, you see.[8] It could mean, because there are fewer white men in jail that other white men are not arresting them. When really you look at it, that's the way it works. "Black boys and teenagers are seven times more likely to be arrested for the same crime as a white person."

You must understand that the policeman is the law in the community. The policeman carries discretion and makes a decision as to whether he will take someone in or leave someone alone. So with a policeman with a prejudiced or a racist attitude, you're going to see the results of that racism. So if you had seven white boys committing the same crime as seven black boys, you'll see the seven black boys in the jailhouse and, perhaps, just one of the white boys in the jailhouse. Then you'll say, "Well, these boys are seven times more criminal than white boys." You can't do that.

Look at what happened to the Jews over there in Brooklyn![9] The second time they've had a riot. The other time they even got into the police station house and ripped it apart, *wounded* 44 policemen. Yet, had you gone to that jail the next day you would not have been able to count all of those Hasidics who were part of that attack. They would not have been in the statistics and you would make the assumption they must be very law-abiding. These people even attacked the law and the law enforcers, but if you go by statistics you're going to be misled. "Oh, they must be very law-abiding people and they must be so self-contained and so forth." This is the game; and we get so psyched out by the game. We must thus be careful about that when we look at these statistics in terms of our males, why you've got to look at it in terms of the political/social situation, or else you're going to misunderstand your own circumstance.[10]

On a given day, the report continued, one in four African American men are under the control of New York's criminal justice system, two times more than all full-time black male college student enrollees in the state. The report entitled "Imprisoned Generation" noted that New York's jail population has gone from 12,500 in 1973 to more than 54,000 today.

It reminds me of a thing I've told audiences before. You thought your problems were going to be solved by appointing more blacks to judgeships, didn't you? I told you, the more black judges you get the more your young men are going to jail. The same things are going to happen with police too. The solution is not the appointing of black judges and police; you've to go much deeper than that. So now we've gotten mayors elected, we've gotten governors elected, representatives elected, I'll bet you there's a monotonic relationship between those numbers elected and the number of black men in jail.

I talk about in this book what I call the *American dilemma*. How do you oppress a people, maintain their oppression, and at the same time appear to be liberal and appear to be working in their interest? You've got to check out that trick-bag because you're going to see the more our men and women are elevated to the jobs in this society, the more they are going to jail, the more they are going to get AIDS, the more they are going to be homeless. Look at it. But when they make you live *vicariously*, through the success of others instead of your own, you are then supposed to be happy when some guy makes a big salary — even though you're still starving to death. When one guy gets a job, as a mayor and so on, you're supposed to say, "My, ain't we gone a long way?" We, who?

They have put us in that kind of mentality and know one token is worth a million. "While they got their eyes on the great successes, we are going to be mowing them down from under the bottom and by the time they realize what's going on, it's going to be over. And then we'll *get* the successes." Yeah, they've got their time coming; they're not going to be saved. They are honorary white men right now, but that's gonna be *revoked*. This is what the "Negro" has failed to understand, with this fairy tale leadership we have out here. "And they lived happily ever after. Little white boys and little white girls and little black boys and little black girls, holding hands together. And they lived happily ever after." Who told you that, man? *Regression* takes place in history. People lose in history. History is not all about progressing. People go backwards in history. But that misunderstanding again comes from us buying the American mythology of progress, that things just have to get better. Nonsense. They can get worse and they happen in historical time.

The idea that you will reach a point where little black boys, white girls and all these people are holding hands does not mean that it's going to last forever. Not at all. Yet many of our leaders leave us with this impression: "Once we achieve this great racially mixed society, the great classless society, it's going to go on forever; we are in heaven then." Not at all. In fact, if you're deceived by that concept, you're going to be cut down right in the midst of what you think are your greatest accomplishments.

Remember the Jews were shot down and done in right at the point when they were integrating into German society, where they thought they were really making it. Of course, logically speaking, that is the point where you should do it, right? From a logical viewpoint, this is when people are least prepared to defend themselves. They've let their guards down; they've stopped thinking in terms of their protection; they don't think they have to defend themselves anymore. That's also at the point where the people become a greater threat to the people in power. That's when you get this type of thing occurring,

What we are talking about here is Afrocentric education. I hope you begin to see that we as Afrikan people have very different things to talk about than do Europeans. You've got to have your children to yourself; you can't just hand them over to other people. You've heard me tell you, there's no such thing as standard education, equal education; you've got to get rid of that notion.

> According to the report, 48% of young minority male offenders are in jail with 16% on misdemeanor probation. Contrarily, [which is the way it's got to be] 48% of young white offenders are on misdemeanor probation, but only 18% are in jail.

As a matter of fact, I had a student of mine the other evening who I think worked for some kind of police agency or something and she indicated that they had to provide a major explanation for the arrest of a white woman. If you arrest a white woman you had better have a doggone good reason for doing so or else you were up the creek. Of course, this reminds you of the thing with the Hasidics and the confession of the policeman there. If you came there to arrest a Hasidic, you had to call the supervisor and go through this whole exercise. Often he wouldn't be arrested; he'd be given a summons and the summons would be thrown right there on the ground, or that sitting in that precinct station is a rabbi so that whenever anything ever goes on in that community, he's right there in the car with the cop to mediate the circumstances. This is power: this is the result of power! The major point I'm getting at here is that we see the black male at the very point of impact of this society.

One other thing, this from *The New York Amsterdam News* (November 24, 1990) about this debate on educating black male teens, as it heats up. It's amazing that we sit around and debate these things so much. That's another thing when you become a nation-within-a-nation — you don't seek the authority and permission of another people to do what needs to be done. Why do we need the permission of white people to decide what we need to teach our children? Have you ever thought the absurdity of that? That you have to ask another people what may I teach my child? Yet, this is a part of what this so-called debate is about, our trying to get permission and authorization from another people to teach our children history, to teach our children the knowledge they need to survive as people. And if we don't get it, we don't teach it. This is pure nonsense. So now we get into a vapid debate with these people for the next three or four years, or whatever, which comes to another inconsequential conclusion or checkmate.[11]

> Their plight is underscored [talking about the black males] by a welter of grim statistics again. A black male teenager is six times as likely as a white male teenager to be a victim of homicide. A fourth of black males between the ages of 20 and 29 are in prison or on parole. The unemployment rate for black males between 18 and 26 living in the inner cities is over 50% and increasing daily.

We're going to come back to that in terms of manhood and the importance of work and labor in defining what it means to be a man. What happens to a man's definition of himself as a man when there is no labor or productive work in which he is to engage? There's a direct connection between productivity — work and labor — and masculinity and sense of manhood. Unemployment is not just merely an absence of jobs, but for a people who want to defeat black manhood, this absence of jobs is a part of defeating that manhood and putting it in doubt, particularly when black males have bought their definition of what it means to be a man.

In 1989, 13.8% of black youths 16 to 24 were not enrolled in school and did not have their high school diploma. The majority of these youth were black males. Frank Spradley [out there in Brooklyn, who some of you have heard about, is dealing with this issue]. We are dealing in critical times, he says, and we need some radical measures to rescue our young black males.

I read these excerpts to emphasize the fact that the black male must be given special attention and focus because he is given a negative special attention and focus by the system of oppression under which he lives. To ignore this special focus and special oppression is to endanger the very survival of our people. Therefore, black manhood must be examined since it is in the context of black manhood that the race itself will survive. This race cannot survive without the survival of the black male.[12] *Women*, you can't do it by yourself. It's not going to happen that way. Your enemy knows it, that's why he has chosen this black male to come after, and destroy, if possible. That is why he has psyched some of the females out, into thinking they can live without him.[13] When you're psyched into that kind of thing you become an ally of oppression.

This in part is what Shaharazad Ali is trying to get at.[14] How does the black woman, in accepting uncritically the values and orientations of an oppressive system, in effect then become a part of the problem of the black male and not a solution to the problem as such. It's got to be looked at. I know it gets at your feminine ego, but you've got to deal with it because it's not about your ego — it's about the survival of a group. We have to put all of our egos behind us (male and female) when it comes to the survival of the group. We've got to get out of defensive postures and all such. How it hurts our pride is not the point, but how do we survive as a people.

So what do we have here? To a good extent a good deal of the material we have been talking about is from this book, *Manhood in the Making: Cultural Concepts of Masculinity* by David Gilmore. You might want to check some of it out It has some good pieces on Afrikan manhood, culture, and what that is about. I think we should read some of this material. I tell my psychology majors that their education is not complete without a working knowledge of anthropology. We underestimate the wisdom of our ancient cultures and the wisdom of our *so-called* primitive cultures severely. Just because a philosophy or ideology occurs later in time does not mean that philosophy or ideology is an advance over older ones.[15]

I think if you really took time and read anthropological studies of Afrikan people, you'd be just so pleasantly surprised at the wisdom contained in their ideologies and how complex the ideologies are; how they solved problems that we see as our most irresolvable today and see the variety of solutions they provide for us.[16] We need to study those cultures. It doesn't matter if they are written by white men, there's a lot of stuff that slips through, there's a lot of stuff there that you can use. Don't let the idea that it's written by a white anthropologist throw you. These folks are blind to many things, too. Even though they may have intentions and other things, even in their blindness they supply you with knowledge and information they don't even know they're supplying you with. You can't go off on a reactionary trip and assume just because something is written by a white anthropologist that it's not of any value to you. You can find stuff of immense value in anthropological works. They may have used it to embarrass us or do things like that, but it doesn't mean that the material cannot be used to uplift at the same time.

Intentionality

One of the reasons I talk against so-called equal education is the fact that education is the result to a great extent of what the student *brings* to the educational process. It is the result of the intentionality of the student. It is intentionality that makes the difference in what you get from education, not what is stated in the classroom. A black student and a white student sitting in the same classroom, one intending to rule, master and control the world gets a very different bit of information, a very different orientation from the same information that is given to the black student. The idea that your children are getting the same education as the white child — when their motivations and values are different, where they want to go and what they want to do with the knowledge are different — is a fallacy. You can't have equal education with people who have different intentionalities. *The* intentionality, whether you intend to be a slave; whether you intend to be a servant; a second banana, subordinated; whether your highest goal is to work for a white man or work for yourself — those things have effects on your memory, they have effects on your perception, on *you* understanding what you're reading and how you apply what you read and know. There is more to education than the handing out of information, its memorization and regurgitation. The student makes the difference in what happens to education. That student, coming from a culture, makes a difference as well. It is not so much that the white man writes it; it is not that as much as what *you* intend to do with it. You'd be surprised when you come in with that Afrocentric intention, when you come in with the intention to be liberated, when you come in as a man and mean not to be bossed by any other doggone man on this earth, then you're going to get a whole different set of information out of the material. But if you want to depend on being "liked," "accepted" and all of that, you're going to be even shy to talk about it. "I don't want to talk about *them* people, they don't wear clothes," or some other kind of nonsense. No! These people have sophisticated philosophies and they can represent many solutions.

Mate Selecting and Societal Mandates

Regardless of the normalities and distinctions made, society still distinguishes between males and females, man and woman, no matter how you play it. Despite all the unisexism, feminism and so forth, a woman marries a man and a woman wants a man. You're not running out here —women—looking for a unisex, are you? You're looking for a man and a man looks for a woman, no matter how you play it and no matter how it works. This is not to denigrate female equality and so forth, but there is still a distinction between these two groups, male and female. We have to deal with that and it's going to be with us for quite some time yet. Societies, all of them, have figured some way of what is appropriate behavior to these two people of the species, no matter how you play it. You can cover it up any way you feel like, but it's still there.

Manhood is something that is different from anatomy. This is the thing you have to keep in mind about manhood. Manhood is a concept that must *constantly* be defined and restructured. There must be a constant dialectic between men and women as to what a man is and as to what a woman is. It's key. You must recognize the definition of what it means to be a man and a woman is the key to the adaptation and survival of a people. It's not merely related to how you deal with each other in your own private home: it's related to the very survival of the race.

Embryology: Let Us Make Male

One thing you have to recognize about manhood to a greater degree than womanhood is that manhood, on a certain level, is an artificial creation as such. In other words, there has to be something added. It is not enough for a man to come into the world with a penis. We don't just call a man "*a man*" simply because he has a penis, saying "He's a male, therefore he's a man." You hear people: "Act like a man! Be a man!" If being a man and having a penis were coterminous, then you could say, "Well, I am a man; I have a penis. So what's the problem?" But you hear women say, "Act like a man! Be a man!" There is something there that goes beyond the anatomy of maleness; there is something to be added onto. In fact, it becomes interesting when you look at the embryology of the human being, you look within the first seven weeks of fetal development and recognize that in the human fetus there are both organ systems present in the body. Nature is very economical. In a way it has only *one* body, and the *basic* body is *female*. You might say. It is basically bisexual. It doesn't waste its time making two separate bodies; it takes one and decides to go one way with it or go the other way with it. You get a body then that has both sets of glands in it, the mullein female glands and the wolffian male glands in the same body. It will be the presence of the male gonad (if it's to be a genetic male) that will determine in which direction that body is going to go in terms of its internal development.

If the testes are there during the first seven weeks, the testes release the appropriate hormones (the androgen or male hormone, another being the mullerian-inhibiting hormone). The mullerian gland that is present in that bi-sexual body, if it were not inhibited by the male hormones would then develop into parts of the female vagina, uterus, and fallopian tubes. In fact, you get a hermaphroditic situation where this sometimes occurs when the testicle operates only one side of the body. So you may have in a sense only a half uterus on one side, with the male side on the other. The male gland hormone, then, inhibits the growth of the female side and stimulates the development of the wolffian glands which develops into the *vas deferens*, the seminal vesicles and the ejaculatory system of the male. If a genetic male's body is not responsive to the androgens, then even though the male's body is a genetic male body, the body will actually develop along the female route. In other words, it will literally stay female in its basic design and configuration. In other words, you need to add something to get the male. If nothing is added, you get the female body. This deals, of course, with the internal sexual organs and systems.

When you look at the external sexual organs and systems you will see that the external organs, too, develop from one organ—the genital cubical on the outside. Both the female clitoris and the male penis will develop from the same bud. Both lips of the female vagina, major and minor, will develop from the same basic slit and what becomes the female lips will in the male become the scrotum sac for the testes. You can see nature taking the same basic body and—depending on the genetic program—using and transforming that body to suit the genetic program; again, an adding on, a plus in terms of the male. If that genetic male body is not responsive to the androgens and so forth—even though it is genetically de-signed to do so—you'll find a body that will stay basically female in its configuration.

I'm going through this explanation to indicate that perhaps, coincidentally, we kind of have this situation even on the sociological/psychological level. Whereas we tend to accept the womaness or femaleness of a woman based on her biological apparatus, we tend not to be so quick to accept the maleness or man-ness of man based on his biological equip-ment. He has to *add* something to it. In other words, manhood is a created product: it is made and developed. That is why in every society you're going to find males at some point taken out for special treatment. Not that females are not, but I'm speaking here of male treatment. In this culture here, we have a lot of people getting upset when we talk about educating the black males, the very idea that at some point they would be separate from black females frightens a lot of folks. I don't know why. If you talk about Afrikan tradition, you should be used to that concept. Black males have been separated from black females for years at a time.

I'll talk to you in a minute about the Samburu, where the black male stays separated from the black female for twelve years, essentially during their education. The Masai endure a similar separation in place and time. You can go from one Afrikan tribe and group to the other: the Afrikan male is separated so that he can be taught the appropriate behavior relevant to the survival of the group and the society and be taught how to relate to women. We'll come back to that shortly.

One of the major problems with this society is that men and women are not prepared to live with each other. You send your children to school and they learn math, science, all this other stuff and they learn everything but the very basic things that make people happy — how to live one with the other; how to be happy, one with the other. No courses on family, no courses on what it means to be a husband, on what it means to be a wife; no courses on how do you get along and resolve problems and issues within your family; no courses in terms of community relations and practicing community relations. Then you wonder why this society is so disorganized and destroyed.

The older systems had the wisdom. They knew that you just couldn't throw men and women together without any training or preparation and just say "good luck." Yet, here this so-called advanced society will teach everything but what it takes for people to live together. Advanced? This is regression. That's why the divorce rate is so bad; that's why the family situation is the way it is and so forth. You must prepare men to live with women. Sometimes the best preparation requires that they be separated for a while so they can have some honest conversation and deal with each other in honesty.

Men and women are like black folk and white folk; you can see the whole psychology of black people change when white folk come into the room. They get uptight; they get embarrassed; we don't want to put the "laundry" out; we want to look our best. Speaking of this, I recall Shahrazad Ali on Donahue where this black woman stood up during the show and said, "Black folks, ya'll act nice now. Remember white America is watching. Let's be on our best behavior." So we can't have an honest or deep discussion because white folks are watching, and this often happens when you have men around women at certain points. We have to maintain our masculine ego. So it's difficult to be honest and relate to each other honestly and deal with some issues because we are defensive about our image in front of women—as we need be—and vice-versa. In order to engage in an honest education of the male, there are times when males need to be together and deal with each other straightforwardly. Men do the best job of making men, just as women do the best job of making women. At some point the boy is made into a man by men. We have to bring that back into our equation if we are to survive as a people.

Manhood is *not* a given, it must be developed. The development of the manhood ideal is not just a chauvinistic idea: the development of the manhood ideal has to be imposed on men and men have to conform to that ideal whether they like it or not. A couple of lectures back, when we talked about man being warlike, aggressive and so forth, we had to remind you that most men are not naturally warlike. You have to draft them into the army; you have to make them go to war. They just don't run to the army. If they ran to the army, you wouldn't have to draft them. Most men under combat don't even fight; many soldiers under combat don't even fire. They have special officers who hang in the back to run the men back up to the lines. Contrary to all your myths and all this other stuff, we like to create the impression that all of us are brave, all of us are ready to give our lives. Come on, it doesn't happen that way.[17] In some of the old time armies, literally the men were beaten into battle. In other words, a good officer knows that you have got to be more frightened of him than you are of the enemy. If you weren't, you'd run over him and run back to the back when things got hard. Most men would like to be home with their wives, families, around the farm and the whole bit; rather than be out in the cold, starving and doing other things men have to do.

War is not a pretty game. It may be made to look good when Sly Stallone is spraying bullets all over the place. That's what gets a lot of American people in a lot of trouble, looking at these stupid movies. Rat-a-tat-tat, rat-a-tat-tat, rat-a-tat-tat; "I'm going to kill them all." That ain't the way it works out. War is hell. It's disgusting. People get hurt, people get killed, people are maimed, people get brutalized. People are used, abused and destroyed, not only the soldier himself, but his family, community and other things are destroyed. War is not a playtime activity and most men if they can avoid it do not want to go in it.

Yet the nation must be defended, the race must be saved, the children must be fed, the wives must be protected and sometimes that requires war. That requires the ability for a man to defend his race, his family, and his children. Sometimes it requires stealing. Yeah, that's what war is about— taking away from somebody what they have. We glorify it, don't we? We make it a big deal. Of course we are deceived by words, aren't we?

The white man deceives his thievery behind the word *war*. He deceives the fact that he runs the greatest Mafia operation in the world behind the words "national interest." A lot of us are caught up with the words. He deceives the fact that South America and Central America are his territory—the United States' territory. "It's our territory and we have the right to exploit it in any way we feel like it and the Russians and everybody else better stay out. You try to get in our special territory (never mind what the people have to say about it)! They don't have a damn thing to say about it."[18] It matters not what the Central Americans and South Americans have to say. It doesn't matter that the Nicaraguans want to elect the Sandinistas or that the Chileans want to put Salvador Allende in office or that the Grenadians wanted Maurice Bishop in office. "No, this is *our* territory!" How different is that from the crack dealer who says, "South Queens is our territory and everybody else stay out?" The people who live there are saying, "We don't want any of you in here." "Shut up, you ain't got nothing to say about it and if you object we are going to get you."[19]

We are willing to see the criminality and the gangsterism there but we don't see the criminality and gangsterism in this country saying, "Central and South America is our sphere of influence." What do you mean sphere of influence? "We collect from this group of people and we make them pay _protection_. Those people who don't agree with what we're doing, we're going to put an insurrectionary army in there and destroy them, or as in Panama, we'll go in and do it ourselves." This is what it's about. What do they mean by national interests or as President Bush says, "Our way of life? The life to which we have become accustomed." That which requires we become a subordinated people.[20] He's letting Saddam Hussein know that we're used to living it up, having more than we can eat, just consuming all of the world's resources and so forth. "I'll be damned if we're going to let you have control of your own resources, no way! We're going to have to fight you if you oppose us." On a certain basic level this is, in part, what manhood and peoplehood is about. Are the people to voluntarily starve and die or are the men to go out and get what is needed for the survival of our people? Are we going to let another people come in and take everything that we have so that our children can starve and die, or are the men going to stand up and defend what they have? This is part of what manhood is about. This is why the men have to be especially psyched up, indoctrinated, and trained. This is why manhood is not a mere chauvinistic definition; it is a social definition. It is supremely related to the people and the survival of a people.[21]

It is not merely a haughty game that men play. In fact, it is a game many men wish they didn't have to play, but they recognize they must because a part of manhood, also, is a *sense of duty*. A part of manhood also is the willingness to sacrifice one's self in the interest of one's people and in the interest of one's folk. That requires stamina, skill, commitment, duty and willingness to put up with a lot of nonsense, hardship, and so forth to see if that is the case. That requires the training of boys —and they have no choice about it. They must be sat up and trained to do it because they not only live for themselves, they must live for the race and for the group. Without the race and without the group, there is no self. This requires certain disciplines.[22]

One of the things that I recommended you read about is the Samburu (by Gilmore) and their image of what it means to be a worthy man, with a heavy emphasis on economic self-sufficiency and productivity. You have to recognize that in the older systems the definition of manhood was tied up with productivity. With the Samburu, a man is a man that owns something (that is not working for another man). That's the ideal. I ask many of our young men today, "How can you accept the definition that man means to be independent and then see the ultimate goal of your life as working for a white man?" It's a contradiction. You cannot see that as the end point of your life, if you define manhood in terms of independence, if you define manhood in terms of self-control, self-determination. You can't do it and then fall subject to the white man. That's why the very definition of your self requires overthrow of the white man in this world today. You cannot be a full man and be subject to rule by a white man; that's a contradiction in terms. That's why you've got to move the black boy beyond going to school just for jobs. He's going to school to remove this white man as his boss, understand?

One of the reasons why you suffer in these schools is because we do not have transcendent goals —goals that move beyond the individual's own desires and wishes. Education is a transcendent goal. It transcends the individual in that education is concerned ultimately with the ability of a people to survive and a transmitting to the next generation of what it takes to survive. Therefore the education of the individual just does not stop with themselves; it moves beyond the self. But when you make the endpoint of the education of your children merely jobs, then it becomes very difficult for you to motivate the child to really understand why that child is going to school because it doesn't move beyond this.[23] Of course, the system likes to keep us at this point. There must be a transcendent reason that we are here. To own property.

Now this group of people, the Samburu, depend on cattle for their wealth. Cattle is wealth — sheep, goats, a few donkeys and so forth — mostly cattle; it's liquid capital. It is the basis of their prestige and influence. Therefore, to be called a worthy elder or a worthy man is to own and control one's own piece of land or one's own herd and to be no one's servant. This is the ideal of manhood for this group. This may involve their having to rustle their cattle from some other people because a young boy has got to establish himself as a man. That may involve taking back from other people. I know that hurts some of our moral sensitivities, but if it does hurt your moral sensitivity, remember where you got your morality from and who taught it to you.[24] We don't look at that enough.

Alienated Christianity

I have to remind people again and again that Afrikan people did not come into this country as Christians. That's a very important point, embarrassed as you want to be about it, Christians, but you have got to face it. "Afrikans did not come in here worshiping Jesus. They came in here with their own religions and backgrounds. Now, am I attacking your worship of Jesus? I'm not doing that. Keep Jesus, love him; he's real to you. I'm not dealing with that because that's not the point of where I'm going here. The point I'm trying to get at is you may not be worshiping Jesus for the same reason that you were taught to worship Jesus. Those are two different things. Do you understand what I'm trying to get at? In other words, you may be converted by a hypocritical preacher, a shyster minister, and come truly to believe in the reality of Jesus. I'm not questioning your belief in the reality. But your belief in the reality of Jesus does not mean that the shyster preacher is still not using your belief in the reality of Jesus to further his hypocritical programs. Do you understand what I'm saying? In other words, he can take advantage of your innocent and pure belief to rook you, exploit you and use you for his own purposes. That is why you have to go even beyond the pure belief in the reality of your god.[25]

You have to also look at how this so-called reality is presented and for what reason it was presented. You must ask the question: Why did the white man teach the black man Christianity? What did he have to gain from that teaching? You can believe that if he thought teaching black people about Christ would defeat his dominance, he would not have taught it to you. You have to understand that. It's very important. One of the reasons why he taught you this is that as soon as we thought about taking from him what he has taken from us, running a raid on his wealth and taking it back, his morality pops up: "Thou shall not steal."

Any taking from him—no matter the fact that he took it from you in the first place—you're made to feel *unentitled* to what has already been taken from you. A part of his moral teachings was to get you just in that state of mind so that you can't bring it upon yourself to take back what belongs to you. You can do only one of two things: you cannot fight to get back what is yours; you can only fight for the exploiters, as we are doing right over there in Saudi Arabia today. How many of those men and women can we get to turn the guns against the people who most abuse them? The moral system will jump right up and say, "No, you can't do it." We see this kind of game going on.[26]

Character Building

Samburu wealth depends on cattle, thus they are taught how to rustle cattle. They are taught how to be brave; they must. They are given initiation rites which to many of us would appear to be cruel. Here the boys trained for manhood, beginning around age ten or twelve. They are going to be in this training for about twelve years and the first part of this training involves circumcision *without* anesthesia. You can imagine what a twelve or thirteen-year-old boy is going feel when you are circumcising him. If you flinch or make one cry you will not be granted the title of man. As a matter of fact we are going to ostracize you, and your whole family is ostracized and shamed. This is not only done by this group, but by many other groups. His male relatives are sitting right there looking at him and the other people are looking at him and watching. Any flinching and movement is called "to run." He is lost and can't continue; he's out of the running from that point. Cruel? Yes, on certain level, perhaps. But on another level, here is man who's got to learn to live with pain. He's got to learn not to be overcome by the fear of pain. He's got to learn how to face death and not run. It's not just a silly tribal primitive ritual; it's deeply embedded into the very economic, political, and social life of the people themselves. The boys have to be trained to undertake this kind of life.

In a world where there is great scarcity and where things must be achieved through competition, the male must be trained to compete, must be trained to take risks. The life of the community depends on him; it's not just a game of male chauvinism. We are in a competitive system. We hear this all time, don't we? How then are we going to live in a competitive system if we do not train our men to be competitive? To be competitive means to take risks, sometimes enormous risks. To be competitive often means to be able to withstand pain and fear that threatens to overwhelm you. Being competitive means being enduring, persistent.

One of the problems you'll find in many of our black children in school which defines their character is what we call the *lack of persistence*, the inability to stick with a problem and stick with a lesson until they master their lesson. They fall easily to frustration. But in order for us to be ruled we must have *children who give up at the first moment of frustration* or men who must quit as soon as they run into rough territory. But the other men who want to rule must make it rough; they've got to. Or else they can't protect what they have. In order for you to take what they have from them — since it is a society of taking — you've got to learn how to deal with the roughness. This is what this thing is about.

Non-Threatening Men

It's interesting to note when you look at the black politicians you hear this word — non-threatening politician. That's one of these new terms! "In other words, we will elect *Negro* politicians who don't threaten and frighten white folks." So David Dinkins, Douglas Wilder, Norman Rice and they've got a Conservative/Republican Gary Franks elected somewhere up there in Connecticut. Also Andrew Young, since we are talking about the non-threatening black politicians. Isn't that interesting? You know what that means, what I quoted to you a while ago, as a result of non-threatening black politicians and judges? Black men and black people being destroyed.

A man must be threatening, particularly to his enemies. If you don't frighten the enemies of the race, then the enemies are going to come in and take advantage of the race. He must learn then to display his capacity to defend to the death his group, his principles, and his people and — if possible — frighten away his rivals, those who threaten. So anytime you get a group talking about electing non-threatening black men you are getting a group that's getting ready to be raped and taken. That's one of the reasons why we have this parallelism between black men going to jail, the kinds of problems we have and the election of non-threatening black politicians because no one is afraid to mess with their people and deal with their people.

Steadfastness in Manhood Definition

We see in the image of the Samburu man that he is not only hard and steadfast in terms of his own definition of manhood, but his steadfastness is an economical phenomenon as well. In that manhood definition is productivity. In order to be a man you must grow more cattle; in order to be a man you must conquer more territory and build yourself a farm or a ranch. This is not only building for that man as an individual; that is building for his family, for his group. His role of manhood is not only a chauvinistic definition of self; it is an economic, productive definition of self as well.

What would happen if we as black men declared: "In order to be a man, we must own the economic systems of our neighborhood? We don't feel like we are full men when we let Korean men, Arab men, white men and other people stay in the midst of our people and take the wealth of our people. How can we look ourselves in the eye and say that we are men?" When you are afraid to face your enemy, deal with the enemy and define your manhood as the defeat of your enemy, then you're thrown back on yourself. A great deal of "black-on-black violence" — whether it is black men against black men, or black men against women, or black men against themselves in terms of destructive habits, such as addictions — is the result of people who have surrendered to a certain cowardice and have given up the thought that they can overthrow the white man and his rule. They have permitted themselves to fall into a state of despair and fear and therefore now seek to soothe their despair and hurt masculine pride by getting inebriated, high, and finishing off themselves for the enemy, or overcompensating and destroying women and children in the same way. I hope you can begin to see that manhood involves much more than chauvinism. Am I able to get through here?[27]

Man as Producer and Provider

In order for the Samburu to be a man, he must engage in self-denial. That's a part of the deal too. One of the things that a Samburu boy does at a certain point is stand before his mother's and the women's quarters and swear that from this point on he will not eat any food seen (prepared) by the married women. He's saying he's not going to eat any more of his mother's food. Does that mean that he hates women? Not at all. He's saying I'm getting ready to move from the position of consumer and taker into the position of producer. No matter how tempting the food is and how wonderful it is — some of this food is their natural food and the food they love very much — "I'm going to deny myself this until I achieve the ability and capacity to make it for myself and vow to feed my mother, rather than being fed by her. A whole different reversal that is part of the manhood ritual; to move a boy (who is a sucker of milk and feeder from his mother's breast) into the role of producer.

We used to have that in our society, too, in the old days. You would hear a guy say when he was young, "Man, the first thing I'm going to do when I start making money is to buy my mama a house." You don't hear that much anymore, do you? "I'm gonna set my mama up and I'm gonna make her stop working." You don't hear that anymore. What you hear now is, "I'm going to mama's and see can I get something to eat." A whole different ethos going on here.

A part of that ceremony of Samburu and the Masai is that the boy cannot be a man until he kills his first oxen. Then he cuts that oxen and gives the biggest piece to his mother. What is he symbolizing? I AM now the producer and the provider.

Man the Nurturer

As I shall show you later, manhood is a nurturing definition. Men are nurturers and givers to their society. It is only in this deteriorated definition of what it means to be a man, only when we have let this oppression separate us from our tradition, that our men continue to be consumers and takers. It is only the absence of knowledge of our culture that has permitted us to deteriorate to the point where we are today, and the taking in uncritically of feminist philosophy to the point where we doubt and are ashamed to say that we *are* men. We've got to get out of that. Note this about manhood here that's prevalent throughout many Afrikan systems. His worthiness comes not only from accumulating, but from lavish gifting during feasts. Among the Samburu, as example, manhood or masculinity is "a kind of moral invisible hand that guides the activities of self-respecting individuals toward the collective end of capital accumulation."[28] What do we mean here? In other words, if you really want to be a "big man," a truly worthy man, after you accumulate this property, cattle and so on, you give it back. You give a big feast. You just feed people and one of the things you really do is you be the one who eats the least at your feast. The more you are able to make people eat more — and the less you eat — the more of a man you are.[29] We see this parallel in the Masai *moran* of Kenya-Tanzania where this young male must *courageously* rise to become an autonomous herdsman and create disposable wealth

This is why you teach these boys they're not going to eat until they kill their own cattle and if they starve, so be it; what can I tell you! We can't afford you. You must demonstrate your ability as a producer. You demonstrate your ability to enter into self-denial. Not because it makes you a man, but in making you a man you feed the nation, you feed the people.

This black man has been duped by this religion into hating money and hating wealth. I try to tell black people we are wealth-producing people; where do we get this thing here of identifying with poverty? Where do we get this craziness of seeing poorness and goodness as the same thing and seeing virtue in poverty? We had to get it from the other people; it doesn't make any sense. There's no greatness in being poor and poverty-stricken. In fact, there's great sin that flows out of poverty. Look who hits you over the head, rich folk? Are they the ones mugging you out here? Poverty is not automatically virtuous. But, of course, the other folk in order to rob us and keep us poor make us associate virtue with poverty. Somehow we are not supposed to make money.[30]

White Mismanagement Normalized

You've got a bunch of jokers around here, "Yeah, black people are not good at counting. Give it to the Jews, they know what to do with money." How in the hell can the Jews count money more than you? Money is money, that's all. The Jew doesn't have any greater facility with money than you. I told you here some lectures ago that the white man is no better manager of business than we are. What is his advantage? *He only makes you pay for his mistakes.* Do you remember when I told you that, back sometime ago? Hasn't the Savings & Loan crisis shown you that? White men mismanaging the economy, destroying the system, the banks. Are they in jail? Are they paying it back? No, we're going to pay for that. Yet we have this myth that they are better managers of business; that they are this and they are that. We don't take the time to see this because we have not received an Afrikan-centered education that can permit us to look through this nonsense and see what is right in front of our eyes.

We see the mismanagement of the economy all the time, total mismanagement, screwing up. What happens? "Well, we screwed it up this time. Sorry, we got to put you off the job." Yeah, we got to furlough you. We got to make you pay more taxes. This is the game. This is what the game is about; *no calling into question* the leadership of the white male as a businessperson or financial person at all. In fact, we think he's even greater now that he sits up and outlines how many jobs must be lost in the city and how many departments cut. He talks percentages and so forth, not realizing that he's covering up his failures. "Oh, but isn't he magnificent the way he lays out how many folk got to be fired and destroyed. Wow, I wonder if a black man could do that?" Craziness, but that's the result of power. You make *other* people pay for your mistakes.

That's the result of weakness; *you* pay for the mistakes of others. That's what the game is about. That's the reality of life. It's not pretty, but that's what it's about.[31]

Feminized Power Masquerading as Strength

A man doesn't worry about being pretty. He has to deal with the harsh realities that exist out here; those realities are not beautiful. Therefore, he doesn't spend all his time primping and going through all of the changes. His duties lie elsewhere. He doesn't get his way in the world through seduction and through the other games. He gets his way through power and strength. The black man has been feminized by the white man. Integrationism is a feminist orientation. "Let us marry the white man. Let us and the white man be as one. And once he sees that I'm his brother and we're the same—there's no difference between us (even though we're as black as seven midnights) —he will now share all his wealth." That's the craziness that animates the assimilationist ideal. Oh, don't worry about building a system yourself. Don't worry about constructing an economic system, a political system and so forth. Just marry the white man and you've got it; it comes with the whole thing. Don't worry about having to fight and struggle to the death with this other person, just marry them. Get them to like you, get them to love you, get them to see you as one with themselves and you got it made."[32] You've got the attitude that all you've got to do is make yourself likeable and you'll seduce them, make them feel guilty. "Ain't you sorry for what you did to us?" We get into that. "Look at all this SLAVERY you put us through. We're weak and broken, don't you feel sorry? Give us 'sumpin fer it'." No, it ain't gonna work that way.

Biblical Tales and Promises as Manhood Preparation

Another thing for you Christian folk and the other religionists (we aren't being prejudiced here). There is a telling illustration of when the rich man comes to Jesus and says,

"What must I do to be saved?" Jesus says, "Give all that money you stole — back." It is interesting what that paradigm represents. Those of us who are Christian, of course, see Jesus as God. Isn't it interesting that this human being comes to God, looks God in the face and when God tells him what to do he says, "Screw you." Did he give his wealth back? No, he didn't. He went right on about his business. What did God say? "It's as easy for a rich man to get into heaven as a camel to get through the eye of a needle." *But the guy was still gone with the money.* What does that say to you, then? If a rich man can look God in the face and say I ain't giving it back, what the hell do you think he's going to tell you?

So you think through some guile and nonsense you're going to rook this white man into giving you his wealth? Through some *moral suasion.* Are you kidding? You're out of your mind. That's not the way it works in real life, ladies and gentlemen.[33]

Men defy God. If they defy God, they damn sure are going to defy you. If you sit around one day waiting for this white man to reach some kind of moral sainthood and share this wealth, you're going to be waiting forever; it's not going to happen. It's not going to go that way. Read your Bible carefully. Move beyond what the preacher tells you sometimes. You've heard me with the Moses story. God promised them the land. Moses gets right there at the Promised Land. Did God give him the key and say, "Here Moses, unlock the gate and go right on in; I promised it to you." He didn't do it. "You go over there and do intelligence in that country. See how it's laid out and so forth, see where the army is, see how the cities are organized." Why are you going to do that? "Because you're going to have to *take* it *by war*, even though I have *promised* it to you." Do you understand what I'm saying, ladies and gentlemen? Simply because something is promised, it does not mean you don't have to *fight* for it. You see that in the Moses story. "I promised you the land and yet I'm not going to give it to you. You're going to have to fight for it."

You're familiar with how they were psyched out over there. "Oh, we can't beat them, they're giants, they're invincible. We were better off under slavery: *take us back to Egypt!*" They nearly hung Moses that night. Read the verse! There, screaming and hollering in the night! "What can we do?" What happened? The ones that were psyched out were condemned to die, stay in the wilderness, stay in confusion, stay in madness — and die. *Only* those who believed the impossible and thought the impossible, that HE is not invincible: *The white man is not invincible!* Do you understand? You *must* understand this. The white man can be defeated — and *defeated by Black men.* If you don't believe it, you're going to die in these gutters with CRACK (cocaine) up your nostrils, which is what is happening to a lot of us already. Those who have given up; those who are afraid they can't change the world; those who have not dared to challenge, to put their lives on the line, they end up dying *anyway*, miserable cowardly deaths. Not only do they end up dying themselves — which we wouldn't mind so much — they take a whole lot of other people with them and destroy a whole lot of other potential who could move us forward as a people. They bought the idea that *the man* is invincible and that they cannot overcome him. Now they die in the wilderness of North America and around the world.

Afrikan Education in Imperialist Schools

We're going to have to bring it to an end, but we have to understand manhood and its relationships. Manhood is also related to generosity. In order for a man to be generous, he must accumulate; he must have something to give away. He must be trained then, to get things. He cannot be trained to be a dependent: he must be trained toward independence. When you see my book, *On the Education of Black Children*, you're going to see a whole list of cognitive styles that have been made to characterize black children. These are some of the reasons they have so much trouble in this educational system.

You must understand that the imperialist mind operates on a very different set of values than the subjective mind. One of the major reasons we have problems in these schools is that we are in schools designed *by* imperialists *for* imperialists and we are subject people in them. We cannot fathom the kind of thinking that is projected in those schools. We cannot fathom why they teach what they teach or why they teach it the way they teach it. We don't see in any way it being related to where we are and where we want to go. It is not. Those schools are designed to maintain *their* dominance and that dominance must be maintained by particular ways of thinking, relating to each other, and particular ways of seeing the world. Now, unless you intend to be an imperialist yourself, or remove imperialists, then the thought styles and approaches they are teaching in these schools make no sense and you will have difficulty learning and developing them. That's a major part of the problem.

"Why am I learning mathematics? Why should I learn to understand English very well?" You don't see it now. You don't see the power of the word, how the word is used in thinking, how the word is used by others, so that you can discern deception from truth and so forth. You're learning this, not because you're trying to be like white folk (that's the last person you want to be like), not simply because you're trying to get a job, but because it is a very part of your capacity to defend yourself.

If you can't understand intent behind a word, motivation behind a word, how a word is being used to manipulate consciousness and so forth, you will be victimized by those words. Consequently, you learn English and the other stuff as a way of self-defense and as a way of moving one's self out from under domination. This is what it's about. You'll see that this imperialist mind is represented throughout the very structure of the schools themselves, all the way through. They are represented in the very thought styles of the white middle class, in contrast to the black middle class and, in particular, to the black lower socioeconomic class. So you will get these differentiations, one being analytical thinking and the other being relational thinking. (I don't have time to fully explain these today). You'll see while one succeeds in school, the other one drops out.

These people have got it all figured out. Look in Janice Hale-Benson's book about the black child. Look at how they show the analytic thinker with high IQ, high success in school and so forth; the analytical thinker, high information and so forth. The relational thinker, trouble in school; the relational thinker, low information, drop-out, behavior problems and the whole range. Yet, if you look at the nature of domination you will see that very thought style is inculcated by the very structure and nature of domination itself; you'll see how it's built in. That's why you've got to be conscious of it or you'll identify it with *"negro"* culture : "That's the way we think, we're intuitive." Yes, we are intuitive, but we are more than intuitive. We are intuitive *plus*! "We're spiritual." Yes, we are spiritual, but we are also analytical. Some of us want to back off and say, "Well, to be Afrikan is to be spiritual, to be intuitive, to be emotional." Come on now, you've got more than that in our head and you have to use both of them for survival. And you have to learn which side is appropriate under what circumstance.[34]

You can't hide behind Afrikan intuitiveness while you're being destroyed. If it's necessary for us to learn how to think analytically, we must learn that style of thinking. Does it mean giving up the Afrikan intuition? Not at all. It means adding it onto our intuition and becoming more powerful than all the other one-sided people in the world. Thus, a combining and a developing into a bi-modal, both sides of the head kind of person, as against the one-sided white man and the one-sided other man there. You'll see these styles are built right in, impulsive style against the reflective style; one that takes time and thinks, the other that just gives you the first answer that comes into their head. This is what it's about.

Afrikan Culture and Self-Mastery as Immunizing Impetus

A major part of manhood training is *self-mastery*. If you are an impulsive type, you can't control your feelings. You're going to rape and rob your own people; you're not going to consume your own people's productions and so forth. You're not going to take time out to process strategy so you can defend your people, family and so forth. You are going to then intake drugs, because you're so impulsive you don't take time to think. There's a direct connection between impulsive orientations and drug addictions.

What is culture? Culture is not merely a knowledge of song and dance, the way we dress and behave; that's very superficial. Culture is a way of thinking. It is an intellectual system. It is a system of self-control. It is the psychic system which subjects impulses and stuff to examination and subjects impulses and desires to evaluation in terms of long-term goals. You say, "I would like this, but in terms of where I want to go I won't indulge myself at this time. Let me delay gratification." But people without culture, people whose very self-definition is not in line with long-term social goals and transcendent values are people who have no reason not to take a drug. They can't give themselves a reason. "Well, why not? What have I got to lose?" He can't give himself a reason. But culture gives him a reason. It gives him a long-term goal and it gives him a comparative system. "This is not compatible with where I want to go. This is going to take me off my path. I will lose my honor and so forth if I go this way. This is not compatible with the survival of my people. This not compatible with taking care of my family. This is not compatible for producing for my group and so forth. I want to real bad, but I'm going to forsake it." How do you do that? You train the young boy to resist temptation; you train him to master his impulses. You train him and make him know that *being a man is the mastery of impulses.* You not only let him know it is the mastery of impulses and spontaneous erratic behavior, but a mastery of knowledge as well—a mastery of systems. That is why manhood and competence are related one to the other in a very definite sort of way. You must be competent and efficient.

If you think this training of manhood only applies where life is harsh or where there are patriarchal differences between men and women, you're not correct in that regard. You still get severe manhood training even in groups such as !Kung Bushmen who have been noted for their egalitarianism, non-sexism and so forth. There, you still get a very similar type of training for the male. So the idea that your men are being taught this therefore they can rule over and abuse women is incorrect; it is not set up for that reason. We have empirical evidence that indicates otherwise and we have Afrikan people who demonstrate this, so we don't have to go through a lot of abstraction. We look at our own people for our need to know.

Through the act of *self-denial* the boy enacts a personal transformation from receiver to giver of sustenance. For the Samburu the idea of manhood contains also the idea of the tribe. When a man defends his honor, if he is identified with his group in the defense of his honor, he is also defending his group. You insult my group, you insult my manhood. I take it personally. It is not a personal aggrandizement, but it is a part of the social role that the man must play.

A part of educating these boys is to educate their identity as men into an identical situation with their identity as Afrikans, so that an attack on Afrikans is an attack on him. This is why the need to separate him for a while. One of the things that oppression has done is to split off the concept of black malehood and manhood from the concept of Afrika. Once they do that, we can see Afrikan people destroyed and feel no real personal insult, no anger and no desire to end this kind of thing.

Alienated Love

This is one of the reasons why we have problems with love, why we are afraid of love. Yes, many of us are afraid of love and in the next lecture I'm going to talk to you about male/female relations in terms of alienation. Alienation is a major problem; man being alienated from himself and women being alienated from herself. In part, Ali is talking about the alienated woman, cut off from herself, making demands that are unrealistic. We have to look, too, at this alienated man. "I don't see color." We have a lot of jokers out here like that. But you know that's an excuse? It translates as, I don't want to identify with my blackness; therefore, I don't identify with their pain, destruction, hurt and I don't take any *personal* responsibility for defending our people against it — as long as I don't see us as black or white, just as human beings! So when they're killing this bunch of people over here: "Well, that's just human beings killing human beings, what can I tell you?" You can't have love, you can't afford love because you can't see people you love being abused, hurt and destroyed. Therefore, if you're afraid of annihilation and self-destruction you have to be afraid of loving and loving deeply. You can't afford to love your people, because in loving them you must come to their defense; in coming to their defense, you must confront their enemies; and in confronting their enemies, you must confront *death*. If you are frightened of all of these, then you are frightened of love. That's a part of our problem.

The inability to love is conditioned by the political/social situation. It's not just personal. It's not, "If you men would just do this" or "If you women just do that." No, you must start from the political/social context and work it into this. Often what we do is start at the wrong level of analysis and it gets into an accusatory, defensive fight and no problem is solved. We have to start it at the right level.

> The idea of manhood contains the idea of tribe, an idea grounded in a moral courage based on commitment to collective goals. Their construction of manhood encompasses not only physical strength or bravery but also a moral beauty construed as selfless devotion to national identity.[35] [... a man whose word is his bond, reliability, and commitment.]

I'm telling you, the major problem in the economic development of our people right now has to be our ability to trust each other and be reliable in our relationships with one another. In order for this system to survive, *we* must exist in a state of *chronic* suspiciousness of each other, a state of chronic doubt about the motivations of each other, a state of chronic fear of reliability in terms of each other. That's why I tell you that every characteristic we complain about among black people has an economic function; it is not just a psycho-pathology. It is put into the black mind to maintain an economic system. The more we are suspicious of each other, the more we don't trust each other, the more we are unreliable in our relationships with each other, the more we don't take our own words seriously. "Oh, well you know you told me you were going to do this?" "Well, I lied." That's a popular phrase now. That ends that.

Elements of Manhood in Afrocentric Education
The more we do that, the less we are going to be able to economically support and liberate ourselves as a people. That's a part of the Afrikan-centered curricula. This ability to trust, to cooperate and be reliable must be consciously taught to our children. It must be a conscious and an exercised part of the education of black children. That's why you can't mix your children in with these other people because you need to teach some very specific things that the other people have taken care of already. Things have got to be put back into our personalities that only we can do and we need to do. The others are not going to do it; they don't even see it as a problem, because it's not a problem with their people. That's what happens when you let another people call what they're about *standard education*.

When you look at these styles of thinking that I will describe in the forthcoming book, these are styles of thinking that have been created by imperialism and so forth. But when you look in the books on educational psychology and so forth, you're not going to see that discussed. So the teacher goes in expecting the child to be able to think in particular kinds of directions. When they don't see that in our children, now we enter into the language of deficiencies, defects and all the other deficits. Again, they deceive us and try to make us think that the school is a non-political instrument and it's not a part of the total political system.[36]

When you really see how the mentality is created then you realize how the children must be taught. The failure of black children in these schools has nothing to do with an absence of intelligence; it has to do with the misorganization of the intelligence, a twisting. Our children and our people literally learn to be dumb; we work at it. You know why we work at it? We've been made to think that being dumb is the result of the fact that our life depends on it. When we grew up years ago and white man called you a "smart nigger," you knew you were in trouble. The one thing he hated more than anything else was a "smart nigger". A smart black man, he was ready to kill him right there on the spot. He had to either subvert that man to working for him, destroy that man's intelligence, or destroy that man's ability to use that intelligence for the advancement of black people. So a lot of us learned the lesson quickly, didn't we? "No, I'm gonna get hurt being smart. I'm gonna be dumb. I'm gonna work at it, too. I ain't gonna listen to nothing you say. I'm not going to let you make me learn anything, because that may make me unpopular with the master." So we work hard at it. You make sure you can shut down when the teacher is trying to tell you something worthwhile.

Manhood as a Family Consensus Definition

We return to Gilmore:

> [Manhood] embodies the central understanding that the man is only the sum of what he has achieved and what he has achieved is nothing more or less than what he leaves behind.[37]

> We may regard "real" manhood as an inducement for high performance in social struggle for scarce resources, a code of conduct that advances collective interests by overcoming inner inhibitions.[38] Manhood ideologies are adaptations to social environments.[39]

Thus, if there is not enough to go around then, men must be trained to struggle for these resources, or we will just voluntarily die and starve to death. This is very important for us to understand. This is why manhood has to be defined again and again. You have to look at the social environment that you exist in and ask, "What kind of man, what kind of woman, does it take to adapt and cope with this environment." That's why, even for the Afrocentrist, you can't get stuck on the Afrikan definition of manhood, one that's stuck back in time. You still have to bring that up to date and ask the question: "What are the circumstances under which we exist today and what kind of characteristics must a man have today for us to overcome the situation that we are in?" Once we finish that analysis: "By what means and methods are we then going to inculcate these qualities into our young men so that they can carry on the struggle for the liberation and the protection of the race?" This is where this kind of thing comes from.

The ideology of what it means to be a man is not a personal definition but is inherently a social definition. This is a definition in which the whole group takes part, men, women and everyone. What kind of man do we want today? What kind of man do we need today? It's inefficient for two people to duplicate each other totally. How do we gain from men and women being just alike? That's an inefficient, uneconomical approach; besides you're not going to be that anyway. We have some people who equate difference with inferiority, or sameness with equality. So some women think that in order to be equal with men, they must be men; it ain't that way. To be different doesn't mean one is inferior, to have a different role doesn't imply inferiority at all. But we let other people psyche

us out—those people who are on top, by the way—and feed
that philosophy to us. Often we get a situation where each one
is blocking the other's development or there is needless
duplication in the role, behavior and orientation of the two
people when it would be much more economical, due to
biological and other differences, that the role and the burdens
be split up and dealt with in a coordinated fashion.

> Again and again we find that "real" men are those who give
> more than they take; they serve others. . . . Manhood therefore is
> also a nurturing concept, if we define that term as giving,
> subventing, or other-directed.[40]

We don't have time to talk about it tonight; but a part of
manhood, of course, is to be a great lover. That's part of what
you teach the boys, too; how to make love, how to make a
woman feel good, how to make her enjoy the sexuality and
enjoy it yourself, how to love with responsibility, with a sense
of social responsibility. You don't have to shoot off into a
woman every time you sleep with her in order to gain satisfaction, to gain a sense of intimacy and so forth. The endpoint of
your loving doesn't always have to be the creating of children,
for which you don't want to care. You can teach men that kind
of orientation and behavior. It becomes interesting to see how
many of the Afrikan societies—even when the men are
separated sometimes, where the men are coming together with
the girls—permit some form of sexual activity that does not
end up in unwanted pregnancy and so forth. Again, a control
of sexual capacity and ability. That is also part of the training
as well.

Many women are afraid that if you get the men together
you're going to teach them all kinds of bizarre stuff. Believe
me, ladies and gentlemen, if a man is taught correctly and
taught for manhood, he is a better man for you, not less. When
these boys come out of this training they are now prepared to
be husbands because they know what the role of the husband

is. They are prepared to perform their role as men because they've been taught what that is about. They are taught how to cooperate with other men so that they can maintain an integrated society and system. They are taught the relating to and satisfying of women. They are taught to have many children, but at the same time how to care for those many children. You can have as many wives as you want as long as you can take care of them. Not only materially, but sexually and otherwise. If you can take care of them, satisfy all of them and keep them going, they're yours. If you can't, you can't have them.

The women cooperate with this convention because this is consensus definition; it is not only reached by men. There is a consensus of men and women about what they want in a man. The woman doesn't want a man who has not been appropriately initiated; she doesn't want to be touched by him. That's a part of the motivation, isn't it. "Hey, you get me when you got something." You get her when you demonstrate your capacity to protect, produce, care for and so forth. You get her when you have graduated from the school of manhood. "If you haven't graduated from the school of manhood, you cannot be my husband; you cannot be my lover."

Thrill of Warrior Lover Husband

How many of you feel the *thrill* of a great soldier, of a man who has confronted danger and survived? That man is erotically arousing. They go together. Deal with it. That's the kind of man you want to *father* your children. The survival of the race ultimately depends on the female marrying or being with men who can protect her productions; if she doesn't, the race disappears. So there's almost a natural proclivity for the women to be erotically stimulated and moved toward a man who has demonstrated ability to survive, protect, accumulate, give and so forth. That is a part of the evolutionary mechanism of survival and we have to look at that.

Men nurture their society . . . by bringing home food for both child and mother, by producing children, by dying if necessary in faraway places to provide a safe haven for their people. This, too, is nurturing in the sense of endowing or increasing. However, the necessary personal qualities of this male contribution are paradoxically the exact opposite of what we Westerners normally consider the nurturing personality.[41]

We're talking about Afrikan manhood, which he admires very clearly, as representing the *pure ideal of manhood.* "To support his family, the man must be distant, away hunting or fighting wars." What are we saying here? A man, if he is to defend a nation and a people must — despite the fact that he'd like to spend with his wife all day and all night and would like to stay home under mama and so forth — master that sentimentality. He must not let that kind of sentimentality overrule his need to defend the nation and to defend his people. Am I getting through here?

So a part of the reason sometimes we find a problem with these men — that they're all not rolling in tenderness and so forth — is the dialectic here and the fact that he's dealing with that. He surmises: "If I give it all in, if I come totally under the seduction of the woman, it's not because she's evil or so forth. But I can't let it happen to the point where I neglect even her protection, the protection of the children and ultimately the protection of the race. I must be able at some point to cut it off and move outward from the community. There must be times when I have to learn to live without her for months at a time, if those months I have to be away at war defending the nation and it takes me months to go and get the products and other things necessary to see to the survival of the race."

So there's a conflict there obviously in the male personality. It's one that's never going to be totally resolved, at least at this point; because the male serves not only as your husband or your lover, but he has a social service to perform as well. Therefore, you're going to see a conflict between those things, or a dialectical relationship. Very often, to fulfill the social service he has to sometimes deny the personal service. I'll get back to that in a minute.

You're going to see this issue of apparent distance wrestling also with the issue of closeness and intimacy. One thing he knows though, if he isn't capable of getting away from mama's strings and getting out from under his woman's seductive desires and so forth, that neither he, the woman, or his mother are going to live or survive. So he's got to learn how to deal with that and he's got to learn then to stay away for months. Not because it's his manly ego, but it's required since it's demanded as part of the definition, if you intend for this man to defend family and nation.

> To support his family, the man must be distant, away hunting or fighting wars; to be tender, he must be tough enough to fend off enemies. [How can he be tender if his enemies have wiped him out?] To be generous, he must be selfish enough to amass goods, often by defeating other men; to be gentle he must first be strong, even ruthless in confronting enemies; to love, he must be aggressive enough to court, seduce and "win" a wife.[42]

So we see manhood being connected with a number of things. I won't go through them now, but I just want to wrap up a few statements here in terms of masculine definition.

Masculine Self-Definition as a Social Definition

A man's self-definition is always on some level a social definition. Manhood definition is a set of social attitudes. No matter how you play it, *men*, you still are defining yourself socially. If you decide you are going to withdraw from everything and be totally to yourself and uninvolved, what would happen to the race if every man — or a large percentage of the males — decided that this is what manhood means, withdrawal and uninvolvement? So if you define it that way it's still a social definition, it still has social consequences and so forth. You can't get away from the social consequences of self-definition. There is no total individual man. Man is social, not totally unique and personal.

We cannot let socially unconscious men flourish among us. That's why you've got to train these boys. Another question you want to look at when you read this book is: "What happens to the guys who don't make it?" Many times some of the kids don't make it, but there's a wisdom there. If being a man is to produce, to economically advance the group and so forth and you do not qualify, then you are going to be a consumer. To a great extent this black community is being raped and robbed, to a great extent this black-on-black violence is largely perpetrated by men with a consumer mentality. "I need a BMW, so I got a right to kill ya. I want gold teeth so I got a right to sell poison to your children. I want this, that, this. Therefore, I can kill you, mug you, hurt you; I can do anything. I want to consume." "Oh man, he's a big dude?" Why? Because he can consume; he eats a lot. He buys a lot of junk.

That is what we call in sociology *conspicuous consumption*. It's not only that you must buy, but what you buy must be seen; it must be conspicuous. So when you're riding around in a BMW, people know right away you must be somebody big. It takes too long to explain if you're not dressed right; in fact, they may not even listen to you at that point. So you want to get your point over immediately; the sisters just jump right in then. If you're riding around in a jalopy, you've got to explain yourself. What are we saying here then? We can't have a race of male consumers. This is a part of our problem, right here, in this Afrikan group — MEN *whose primary drive is consumption.* They don't care how it's made, who makes it, just let me get it. The Japanese tried to get through to you and tell you the truth. "Give me an apology," we demanded, instead of mulling over how do you make these doggone things since our kids buy so many of them. If I can make it, then I can sell it to them myself or provide them with it and consequently, they won't have go out and kill and knock people in the head to get it. No, we don't want that; we are so busy reacting to insults! That's the problem with the neurotic; they have misplaced pride. They get upset over the wrong things. It's foolish for a people to buy all these radios and all this garbage and not become producers themselves. Other men have a *right* to question your manhood, peoplehood and sanity when you do that. What kind of crazy people hand Koreans and other people thousands and thousands of dollars while their children go hungry in the street? Dare they call themselves people? It doesn't make any sense. They tell you to your face and because you don't want to accept truth you want to holler about them.[43]

Korean Boycott

This thing about the Korean boycott had nothing to do with the Koreans being nice, smiling or learning the American way of doing business. I don't give a hang about Korean smiling or being nice. The true base of that boycott—while we regret the hurting of Miss Philosant—should go deeper than the mere insult of that woman. We have to be up-front with this: *we want this community back*. We want to use our wealth for our own advancement, our people, and we don't have to apologize to anybody for it. We don't have to fix it up. We don't have to make excuses for supporting our own children with our own money. Screw you if you say it's reverse racism; later for you, we don't care about it! I'm not going to sit down and argue with you over it![44]

Yet we have some people apologizing, going through all kinds of gyrations. You are under no obligation to starve your children for another people. We don't owe the Koreans a living. When are we going to wake up?

Blood Spilling in America's Wars: A Paradox

As I told you before, I have seen black men die on the soil of Korea, die protecting Koreans, going off to war when we were still riding in the back of the buses, going off to war when we were still drinking from separate fountains, going off to war when we were eating out of the back ends of restaurants, ladies and gentlemen. I saw them as a child myself go to war, some who did come back and others who came back in coffins and other things, for rights that Koreans can exercise as soon as they hit the soil of America—rights that they themselves could not exercise.[45] Getting gypped in war after war after war, from the Revolutionary War right onto today. Then what happens? They are still over there today and they're going to die if the Red Chinese or the North Koreans decide to run into South Korea again, black men and women dying—with Koreans over here cheering, 'Go head, go head.' Where are they? What's going on? This is a gyp; this is a sign of people who are unconscious. Then, not only do you fight and die for them, to protect them, people who have a country, *by the way*, a people whose country is exhibiting one of the highest economic growth rates in the world — a people who took *our* tax money.

I often remind people, we forget that we pay taxes. We think the government is giving us white folks' money. This is your money. From slavery all the way up to the income tax; you pay all the time, in every kind of way. So we're supposed to feel grateful as if white folks are giving us something. This is your money, your labor. Do you understand? Yet that money also went to Korea, to build an economy, to build a system there. So here come these people with our tax money in their back pocket, setting up businesses in the black community, to work us *again*. Of course we are told that they are there because they work harder. We believe that nonsense.

You know what I say about America? The best way to get money out of white folk is to fight them. If you fight them in a war, they'll give you the treasury. Look at Japan. We built that economy, too. Black money, black taxes, black men dying built it up and America just can't wait to give them all they've got. Let's do it again; Germany? What did we call that—the Marshall Plan? Taking all the people's money and shipping it, rebuilding England, rebuilding France, rebuilding Germany. Now we're going to rebuild Eastern Europe and the whole bit, *with black folks' money*; or if you're not making it you're out of a job, so that it can be done, one way or the other. Then we permit some folks to come in and say that they're in the position they're in because they work harder. You've got to be out of your mind to go for that—and they've got to think you are crazy for going for it. They can't have respect for you when you fall for that okey-doke, and when you *feel* some compulsion to support them. Some of us would claim, "I don't see color." You don't see anything—you're totally blind!

Crime as Export Patriotism

In this book, *Black-on-Black-Violence*, I talk about the exportation and importation of crime. No time to fully explain it now—about how England, Europe exported its criminals. Often I'd say, if you want to get rid of crime in the black community, take somebody else's community. That's the way the world is set up. These Europeans were so overrun with crime, whorishness, and all else, the society was having a hell of a time. So what do you do? You export the criminals out into the New World and their criminality now becomes *redefined* as patriotism as they kill the Indians. So now, their killing and murderous attitude is transformed into working for the nation.[46] After they get through killing, murdering, raping and robbing, they get access to wealth and they don't have to mug people in the head directly anymore; they have an army and a police force to do that. Then they can pretend they are morally pure. By then, they have wiped out all the Indians anyway. They've increased their wealth, which reduces their necessity to do direct street crime; they can leave that to the other folk now. Of course, they can pretend that they are morally superior since they're not now arrested for street crime. That's because they have committed an even greater crime that now permits them not to have to do that for a living. They let other people do the murdering and the killing and now look morally pure. Not only did they increase their own wealth, they increased the wealth of their mother country; so that they could reduce, relatively speaking, the crime there. In a sense by exporting crime, they reduced their own internal crime.[47]

We have the same thing going on here. The Koreans, by exporting themselves into the black community, we subsidize the Korean youth from being juvenile delinquents. Do you see what I'm saying? They don't have to go out here and knock people in the head because they've got all your money already. But being left without any in our own pockets, we've got to go out and knock somebody in the head. So the Korean is not naturally any more law-abiding than anyone else, but he's run a trick on the black man's mind so that he doesn't have to engage in crime with the type of frequency that we engage in crime.[48] Now, if we kept our own money in our pockets and multiplied that money within ourselves, our children wouldn't have any need to knock people in the head either. But, we're filled with morality. "I don't discriminate. I don't do this." But you create immorality with that kind of so-called moral thinking. You have to understand that the same thought in a different context has a different outcome. Filled with your sanctimonious brotherly love and not "seeing" any difference and so forth means you ignore your own children, your own race, and *feel holy* because you've handed all your money to other people and their children. You are making criminals of your own and destroying your own at the same time. You have created immorality with your morality.

False Morality thieves Black Talents

It's not enough to go in these churches and kick over benches and so forth. You've got to understand what you're being taught, how you're being taught and for what reason you're being taught. You've got to learn to think. You fall victim to all this rhythm, talking in tongues, bellowing and carrying on. That's not religion. The people must be taught, and if the minister's not teaching the minister is mis-serving you. I don't care how "good" you feel. Under oppression every system is turned backwards and that includes the church. In the midst of your greatest religious fervor, if you're not awake to what you're doing, you're actually sowing the seeds of sin and destruction. When you let religion make you feed other people's children, denude yourselves of your own wealth and denude your children of your own heritage, you are not being moral, you are part of the problem. You are an ally of the Devil; I don't care how you cover it up with Bible verses or anything else.

I've told you about the servant in Matthew: 14, with the master who goes away, leaves his servants talents and wants them to increase the wealth that he left them. You get one who is full of excuses; he didn't invest in anything. He was given talents, but he had all kinds of excuses. "I know you reap where you didn't sow." He just carried on, like some of our folks; we just carry on and whine and whine about what white folks did and that's the reason why we can't do anything. What happened to him? The master took from him, even the talents that he had, and gave it to the people who already had talents and who expended it. What did he say? "To him who has, more shall be given."

We say in folklore "the rich get rich and the poor get poorer." That's a solid rule. If the poor are not conscious and awake, they will get poorer because the rich are going to organize their thought and behavior patterns so that they can be separated from the little they have. I've told you the black child is a talented child, the most talented child on this earth, no two ways about it. How much have we invested in this child? If we do not invest in these children then, what little talent they show will be given to other people and be taken from us. What little money they earn will be spent with other people and taken from their own. Black music sells 60% of World Music. Black music outsells national music in many countries; people buy more black music than their own native music. Sixty percent! That's because we are *talented*, we can sing and dance like nobody else in this world, can't we? We can finger-pop and make everybody feel good. But where is the ownership of the music industry? Where is the control of our cultural product? How are we benefitting from our talent? Or is our talent now being taken from us and being given to another people?

The Japanese have utter disdain for us because they own CBS Records, one of the biggest record companies around. They are living off black folk's money, black folk's talent. That's why they express disrespect. Here are a people giving away the talents of their children and themselves by the ton. We brag about how much money we have to spend. "We are the 9th richest nation on earth; we have $360 billion." That's true, but have you ever thought about how much wealth you generate? See, that's your take home pay. If you're taking home $360 billion, how many trillions of dollars are you making for someone else? That's the question. When Muhammad Ali or Mike Tyson earns 10 or 15 million dollars for a boxing match, how many millions do you think that match is creating? You're talking about a match that creates $300 million or more; these guys are getting pennies out of this. Although for us it's, applauded "wow", why not own the whole industry? But this is what happens when you get psyched out.[49] Even that which we have—even the wealth which we could produce—is taken from us, and then we cry about how poor and downtrodden we are, how we're starving to death and how we're suffering out here while we are the greatest wealth-producers this world has ever seen. That's why they like to enslave us; that's why we were enslaved in the first place. We weren't enslaved because they loved us; we were enslaved because *we produced wealth*. Why do you go to work; because they love you; they want to feed your family? You're out of your mind. You produce wealth. As soon as you don't produce wealth, out you go; that's the way this game is set up. Yet, Afrikan people have a tradition of wealth-creation;

we started the wealth-creation business, which I guess is one of the reasons we are so good at it now — in the service of other people.[50]

When you talk about the building of cities in Mesopotamia, that means that there was enough surplus wealth produced so that all of the people did not have to engage in subsistence farming, hunting and so forth. It means the farmers had reached such a level of productivity they could afford to feed people in the city, people in the cities then could engage in various other activities. When you look at the first major cities on this earth — which were Black cities — realize what a city means economically. These were not just people hanging out. Realize what that means economically for a nation to support not just one, but *many* cities.[51]

When you read your Egyptology, do not only get hung up about Heru (Horus) and all the rest of those gods. As I've told you before, you may worship these gods and so forth, but I've never seen a god build a pyramid. I've never seen God build a church either. I see men, women and people put brick by brick to build that thing. God might have inspired them, I don't deny you that. That might be important to the building of the church, I don't argue with that. Certainly that is important to the building. But the actual organizing of the building gang, the actual procurement of the materials, paying of people for their labor, the actual feeding of people, the number of professions that must have been involved in building a building must also be considered. Thus when you say the black man built the pyramids, built cities and so forth and was the first to do so, that is also saying the black man produced enough surplus wealth so this could happen. It is also saying the black man was first to define all types of professions and skills. The people who built pyramids were people with skills; you're talking about craftsmen, masons, architects, supervisors, accountants, scribes, people who are procuring food, people who are building houses. Remember, people have to be housed. Think about the number of economic activities that had to take place in order for that pyramid to be built. Think about the number of economic activities that take place in a city where trade is the main source of living. So when you talk about the firstness of Afrikan civilization, you're not just talking about firstness in terms of pure physical structure and so forth. You're talking about firstness in administration, firstness in professionalism, firstness in skills development, firstness in organization. How in the hell then do you get to this point where you think that being a professional person, being a skilled person, being a wealth-creator is foreign to the Afrikan personality? Isn't it amazing the depths we have come to? We passed on the accounting system and language system to the Semitics, people today you call Jews who inherited this whole accounting system from Afrikan people. This is one of the things we have to reclaim, but we can't reclaim it without the Afrikan culture. You can't claim it until you become an Afrikan; there's no other way it's going to happen. You've been trying to claim it by acting like a white man.

An Afrikan Ideal: The Way Forward

We cannot permit men who place consumption and their own hedonistic desires ahead of race survival to flourish amongst us. They need to be weeded out. They cannot be permitted the status of man within the group. If you allow it, you're headed for destruction. We cannot permit men who cannot master themselves to exercise roles of leadership. We cannot permit black and white feminists to so confuse what it means to be a man until males are left paralyzed by their confusion, caught up trying to figure out who and what they are, afraid to assert themselves. We've got a lot of guys who have this problem; afraid to assert themselves in terms of defining their manhood, at the same time patronizing women and afraid to deal with that. You're not doing the women, nor yourself, any favor. Certainly there are going to be disagreements, certainly there is going to be some tension around those definitions. That is a part of the deal, part of the tension that we have to accept as a part of living. There's always going to be a bit of that. The thing is to have the open-mindedness, the self-control and so forth to enter into dialogue and continue to evolve. But when you try to reach a point where everything is totally resolved and controlled, then you're headed for death. You must accept what is called the *constant job of becoming*, the constant job of development.

The woman must see that in the man's protection of the race, he is also providing for her protection. This is *her* sacrifice for the race. This is in part what Shaharazad Ali is really trying to get at. You cannot let your neurotic drive for security and other things become so overwhelming and so all consuming until the man has no time to attend to the business of the race and the business of protecting the race's interests. This is part of the deal. When women accept their opponent's definition of what it means to be a woman and what are a woman's rights are out of tune with the reality of her group, she then becomes an impediment to the development of the man. A lot of our women — reading *Cosmopolitan* and the others, looking at these television programs and so forth — coming into the marriage demanding that the man do this and that without any regard to the political realities of the situation, become a problem. I've made a quick list of female demands and the next time I come I'll talk to you about it. (That doesn't say that males don't have any.) I think I got up to about 40. I heard a lady on the phone the other day who said, "I wrote down what I ask of a man and I reached 32." Many people are not aware of that. Many women think they are asking you for a simple this or that but are not conscious of what they are really demanding. I bet you when I read this list there won't be one who won't say it's your natural right as a woman as to what a man should do. You'll see that a man has got to be "in love" with you; he's got to be in a state of mind because you don't do anything with people you're not in "love" with. (It goes the other way, of course. Men have demands on women. It helps us if we would enumerate just what demands we make on each other). The woman has a lot of demands on the man; the man has his own self-demands. You can see a conflict.

For instance, first one I list here is *Priority Attention*: "I must be the most important thing in your life, your total obsession." There are severe problems there. Of course, this is popularized in music: "Oh, you know I can't think; I can't live without you; there's nothing else I think about in the world but loving you." Come on, get off of it. You gotta think about some other things. You're not going to even love her right if that's the only thing you think about. She's not going to even be around for you to love after a while if that's the only thing you think about. Do you understand that a man has demands on himself as a person and the society also places demands on him? So there are three sets of demands. What do I owe the woman? What do I owe my self, in terms of the way I see myself? What social obligations do I have? These have got to be balanced off against the reality of the political situation in which the person exists. This is not the same situation as white men. So you can't just say, "You should do this because you're a man." What do you mean? It has to be done within the context of how we as Afrikan people have come to define what a man is and what he does within the reality of our situation today. Once we change that reality, we can change the roles and duties of what it means to be a man. But to throw those things outside of the reality is to throw the relationship into all kinds of problems and trouble and ultimately weaken and destroy the race. That's a part of the situation.

If we could get around Ali's being so defensive (certainly her writing style provokes and certainly there's over-generalization, over-statement and some downright wrong things stated), but that does not ignore the issue that she's trying to deal with, some very pertinent things that we are confronted with as a people. We don't have to spend our time cursing her out and carrying on. We can use it as a stimulus to get into honest dialogue to solve some real problems. You see the same thing with these circuses produced by folks like [Phil]

Donahue, people hollering and screaming at Ali and Ali hollering and screaming back at them and no sensible discussion taking place at all.

A part of the woman's sacrifice for the race is for her to sometimes turn the man loose and for the mother to let her son go sometimes. Even though she may wish to keep him with her at all times, she too must realize the role he must play. She must not let their total selfish desire rule over the total situation. There is a reciprocal interplay and exercise of power between man and woman pivoted around personal needs, family concerns and race survival. The man cannot let the woman's personal demands so overwhelm him until they threaten to destroy the well-being and heritage of the family and of the nation. When they do, the man must exercise his masculine prerogative to put an end to such demands. Now, does he have to slap her in the mouth, as Ali is saying? Not necessarily. But there is a point where if the demands are reaching neurotic proportions and consuming the man's capacity to move himself, his family and the race forward, then the man has to bring an end to that kind of behavior. It has to be stopped.

The woman does not submit to the man. I want you to listen carefully to this, women, because there's a confusion here. The woman does not submit to the man — that's a part of the confusion again with Ali's book; when she talks about submission, the hackles go up — "submitting to a man"(?)! Not to the man, but to the higher ideals he represents at the time. In other words, if the man is truly in line with his culture, truly defined in terms of his culture and acts in terms of his cultural interests, when he prevents a woman's neurotic drives he is not asking her to submit to him as a man but to submit to the ideals of the race, the group, and the nation which he is representing at that point. People confuse the two things. So what happens in the fight? You're concentrating on the man (your submission to the man) and ignore completely the principle or the ideal possibly being projected at that point.

This leads to a lot of fights. People get caught up in all kinds of personal and defensive issues instead of saying let's discuss the problem, let's look at the ideal, let's look at what we're trying to solve here.[52] The problem may not be about me submitting to you or you submitting to me, but submitting to a higher ideal we both represent in our relationship. Let's go the other way then.

When the man stupidly behaves in ways that are destructive to the family and the nation, to the well-being of both, the woman exercises her feminine prerogative and he submits to the higher ideal that she represents. They both respond to the ideals of their culture and their group within the reality in which they exist and they call each other and check each other in terms of those things. Therefore it is not a personal man riding on woman or woman riding on man, but a calling into focus and consciousness a higher thing than you or I — a thing which we both have a consensus about.

This can only happen when both fairly share clearly existing cultural ideals, their relationship arbitrated by such ideals. That means that both men and women should be trained culturally and trained for their goals. When the cultural ideals of a race are destroyed, to whom and to what can you appeal in arbitrating your disputes as people? So the teaching of the black male, and parallel with that is the teaching of the black female, is a very necessary thing. It is very necessary to the very survival of the people. Thank you very much for your attention.

Notes

1. Robert P. Moses (2002). *Radical Educations: Civil Rights from Missis-sippi to the Alegebra Project.* Boston: Beacon Press.
   Isabel C. Barrows (1890). *First Mohonk Conference on the Negro Question* (held at Lake Mohonk, Olster County, New York, on June 4, 5, 6, 1890) Boston: George Ellis.

2. Keith Bradsher, "Low Ranking for Poor American Children. U.S. Youth Among Worst Off in Study of 18 Industrialized Nations." *The New York Times,* 8/14/95, p. A9.

3. Keith Schneider, "Blacks Fighting Blacks on Plan for Dump Site." *The New York Times,* 12/13/93, p. A2.
   Harriet Washington, "Widening Gap in Race-based Pollution." *Emerge.* July/August 1995, p. 19.
   Ronald Brathwaite, Sandra E. Taylor & H.M. Treadwell, eds. *Health Issues in the Black Community,* Hoboken, NJ: Jossey-Bass, 2009.

4. Vince Beiser, "Look for the Prison Label: America Puts its Inmates to Work." *Village Voice,* 5/21/96, pp. 37-40.

5. Richard Kluger (2009). *Simple Justice.* New York: Knopf.
   Theresa Perry, Robert P. Moses, Joanne T. Wynne, Ernesto Cortés, Jr. & Lisa Delpit (Eds.). (2009). *Quality Education as a Constitutional Right: Creating a Grassroots Movement to Transform Public Schools.* Boston: Beacon Press.

6. Mario M. Cuomo (1974). *Forest Hills Diary: The Crisis of Low-Income Housing.* New York: Random House.
   J. Anthony Lukas (1985). *Common Ground: A Turbulent Decade in the Lives of Three American Families.* New York: Knopf.

7. State Senator Alton R. Waldon, Jr. (1995). *Unhealthy Choice: Prisons Over Schools in New York State. How New York State Is Sacrificing Education For Incarceration* (St. Albans, NY 10th District).
   Charshee C.L. McIntyre, *Criminalizing a Race: Free Blacks During Slavery.* New York: Koyode Publications, 1984.

8. "There are three kinds of lies: lies, damn lies and statistics." Leonard H. Cartney, 1895.

9. NYPD Confidential, "Dealing with the Hasidics: Playing with Fire." www://nypdconfidential.com/columns/2006/060410.html. 4/10/06.

10. Rachel Aviv, "The Outcast: After a Hasidic man exposed child abuse in his tight-nit Brooklyn community, he found himself the target of a criminal investigation," *The New Yorker,* 11/10/2014.

11. Ethan Bronner, "Report Shows Urban Pupils Fall Far Short in Basic Skills." *The New York Times*, 1/8/98, p. A12.

12. See Valethia Watkins, "Doing Maat: Reflections on Gender and Justice for All Africans," presented at Association for the Study of Classical African Civilizations'(ASCAC) 32nd Annual Conference, Seattle, Washington, on March 18, 2015. Watkins bemoans the fact when President Obama initiated a program called My Brother's Keeper, he experienced extreme backlash — a 1,000-signature letter by black women feminist academics — for his audacity to help young black men and men of color, yet they did not so object when he created the *White House Council on Women and Girls*, or Michelle's *Let the Girls Learn*, which catered to females exclusively thus excluding all males *irrespective* of needs desperation.

13. Haki Madhubuti (1978). *Enemies: The Clash of Races*. Chicago: Third World Press, 1978.
     _____. (1980). *Black Men: Obsolete, Single, Dangerous? The Afrikan American Family in Transition. Essays in Discovery, Solution, and Hope*. Chicago: Third World Press.

14. Shaharazed Ali, *The Blackman's Guide to Understanding the Blackwoman*. Philadelphia: Civilized Publications, 1989.

15. David D. Gilmore (1990). *Manhood in the Making: Cultural Concepts of Masculinity*. New Haven: Yale University Press.

16. S.K. Damani Agyekum (2012). *Distorted Truths: The Bastardization of Afrikan Cosmology*. New York: Afrikan World InfoSystems.

17. John W. Chambers (ed.). (1973). *Three Generals on War* (comprising) *Old Europe's Suicide*, Brigadier General C.B. Thompson; *War is a Racket*, Major General Smedley D. Butler; and *The Men I Killed*, Brig. Gen. Frank P. Crozier. New York & London: Garland Publishing.
     Lt. Col. Dave Grossman (1995). *On Killing: The Psychological Cost of Learning to Kill in War and Society*. New York: Little, Brown.
     George Carlin talks about the intentional obscuring of language to hide the reluctance of men to fight, i.e. WWI "shell shock", WWII "battle fatigue", Korean War "combat fatigue", Vietnam "post traumatic stress disorder (PTSD) syndrome".

18. George G.M. James (1954). *Stolen Legacy*. San Francisco: Julian Richardson Associates, pp. 21-26.
     Ernest R. May (1975). *The Making of the Monroe Doctrine*. Cambridge, MA: Belknap/Harvard University Press.
     Hugh G. Miller (1929, 1970). *Isthmian Highway: A Review of the Problems of the Caribbean. American Imperialism: Viewpoints of United States Foreign Policy, 1898-1941*. Salem, NH: Ayer Company Pub.

19. *See* John Perkins (2004). *Confession of an Economic Hitman.* Oakland: Berrett-Koehler.

20. Maj. Gen. Smedley D. Butler freely admitted he was a hired thug for US corporations in Central America and other places in the world.

21. Ralph Schoenman (1990). *Iraq and Kuwait: A History Suppressed.* Santa Barbara, CA: Veritas Press.

22. John Whiteclay Chambers, ed. (1973). Introduction. In *Three Generals on War.* New York & London: Garland Publishing, pp. 39-40.

23. Dr. Clarke on The Issue of Multicultural Education stated as follows: "The whole concept of multicultural education is to water down our history, put it on par with theirs and to let us know that they (condescendingly) accept the fact that we did a few things. But when it comes to world civilization , they're the ones that brought it in. But how could they bring it in when Africa was already old? They hadn't even started wearing shoes."
    > *The Family as Nation*
    > The Black Family in America Conference
    > Louisville, Kentucky, on March 8, 1996.

24. Hearken not to Hezikiah: for thus saith the king of Assyria, "Make an agreement with me by a present, and come out to me, and then *eat ye every man of his own vine, and every one of his own fig tree and drink ye every one the waters of his cistern."*
    — Rev. C.I. Scofield, "II Kings, Chapter 18, Verse 31." *The Scofield Reference Bible.* New York: Oxford University Press. 1909, p. 445.

25. The Bible entered England at the end of the sixth century A.D. In 597 the monk Augustine came to that island as a Christian missionary, bringing with him from Rome nine books (all in Latin, of course): a two-volume copy of the Bible, two Psalters, two copies of the Gospels, and three other religious books. These were England's first library.
    — Butler B. Trawick, *The Bible As Literature: Old Testament History and Biography.* New York: Barnes & Noble, Inc., 1963, p. 26.

26. Richard Perez-Pena, "Study Shows New York Has Greatest Income Gap." *New York Times*, 12/17/97, p. 1.

27. JoAnn Gibson Robinson (1987).*The Memoir of JoAnn Gibson Robinson: The Montgomery Bus Boycott and the Woman Who Started It.* Knoxville: The University of Tennessee Press, pp. 36-37.

28. David D. Gilmore, *Manhood in the Making*, p. 133.

29. Giving and sharing as a theme are reflected throughout Afrikan

literature through time. It is especially reflected in the literature of Kemet, "The Hotep Di Nswt" is a primary example. People are always giving. They celebrate people's passing, remarking how generous they were, etc.

Miriam Lichtheim, *Ancient Egyptian Literature, 3 Vol.* (1975). Berkeley / Los Angeles: University of California Press.

Maulana Karenga (1984). *Selections From the Husia: Sacred Wisdom of Ancient Egypt.* Los Angeles: Kawaida Publications.

Asa G. Hilliard, Larry Williams & Nia Damali (1987). *The Teachings of Ptahhotep: The Oldest Book in the World.* Atlanta: Blackwood Press.

30. In those years after the Civil War, a man named Russell Conwell, a graduate of Yale Law School, a minister, and author of best-selling books, gave the same lecture, "Acres of Diamonds," more than five thousand times to audiences across the country, reaching several million people in all. His message was that anyone could get rich if he tried hard enough, that everywhere, if people looked closely, were "acres of diamonds."

A sampling:

I say that you ought to get rich and it is your duty to get rich . . . The who get rich may be the most honest men you find in the community. Let me say here clearly . . . ninety-eight out of one hundred of the rich men of America are honest. That is why they are rich. That is why they are trusted with money. That is why they carry on great enterprises and find plenty of people to work with them. It is because they are honest men. . . .

. . . I sympathize with the poor, but the number of poor who are to be sympathized with is very small. To sympathize with a man whom God has punished for his sins . . . is to do wrong . . . let us remember there is not a poor person in the United States who was not made poor by his own shortcomings . . . .

See also Howard Zinn (1980). *A People's History of the United States.* New York: HarperCollins, p. 256.

31. Lawrie Mifflin, "History Channel Cancels Plan For Series on U.S. Companies." *New York Times,* 6/7/96, p. D4.

32. Steven Lee Myers, "Business Interests Overshadow Human Rights, Survey Reports." *New York Times,* 12/5/96, p. A8.

33. Matthew, Chapter 19: 20-26.

34. Janice Hale-Benson (1986). *The Black Child.* Baltimore: Johns Hopkins University Press.

35. Gilmore, pp. 144-145.

36. Sally Patel, "Psychiatric Apartheid." *Wall Street Journal*, 5/8/96, p. A14.

37. Gilmore, p. 145.

38. Ibid., p. 223.

39. Ibid., p. 224.

40. Ibid., p. 229.

41. Ibid., p. 229.

42. Ibid., p. 230.

43. Vicki Robin, "Poor Nations Call Our Bluff on Consumption." *Newsday*, 10/31/94, p. A27.

44. The economic philosophy of black nationalism is pure and simple. It only means that we should control the economy of our community. Why should white people be running all the stores in our community? Why should white people be running the banks of our community? Why should the economy of our community be in the hands of the white man? Why? If a black man can't move his store into a white community, you tell me why a white man should move his store into a black community? The philosophy of black nationalism involves a re-education program in the black community in regards to economics. Our people have to be made to see that any time you take your dollar out of your community and spend it in a community where you don't live, the community where you live will get poorer and poorer, and the community where you spend your money will get richer and richer. Then you wonder why where you live is always a ghetto or a slum area. And where you and I are concerned, not only do we lose it when we spend it out of the community, but the white man has got all our stores in the community tied up; so that though we spend it in the community, at sundown the man who runs the store takes it over across town somewhere. He's got us in a vise.

So the economic philosophy of black nationalism means in every church, in every civic organization, in every fraternal order, it's time now for our people to become conscious of the importance of controlling the economy our community. If we own the stores, if we operate the businesses, if we try and establish some industry in our own community, then we're developing for our own kind. Once you gain control of the economy of your own community, then you don't have to picket and boycott and beg come cracker downtown for a job in his business.

— *Malcolm X Speaks: Selected Speeches and Statements.* "Ballot or the Bullet." New York: Grove Press, 1965, pp. 38-39.

45. As long as the white man sent you to Korea, you bled. He sent you to Germany, you bled. He sent you to the South Pacific to fight the Japanese, you bled. You bleed for white people, but when it comes to seeing your own churches being bombed and little black girls murdered, you haven't got any blood. You bleed when the white man says bleed; you bite when the white man says bite; and you bark when the white man says bark. I hate to say this about us, but it's true. How are you going to be nonviolent in Mississippi, as violent as you were in Korea?
— *Malcolm X Speaks: Selected Speeches and Statements.* "Message to the Grassroots." (Ibid.), p. 7.

46. J.A. Rogers (1961). "The Pilgrims as Drunks and Sodomites" in *Africa's Gift To America: The Afro American in the Making and Saving of the United States.* New York: Helga M. Rogers, pp. 33-34.
Iskakamusa Barashango (1980). *Afrikan People and European Holidays, Bk 1.* Washington, DC: IV Dynasty Publishing.
Robert Hughes (1987). *The Fatal Shore: The Epic of Australia's Founding.* New York: Alfred A. Knopf.
Howard Zinn (1980, 1990). *A People's History of the United States.*
Kevin Phillips (1998). *The Cousins: The War, Religion and Politics and the Triumph of Anglo-America.* Also *see* Professor William Mackey's and Professor J. H. Clarke's lectures.

47. Prof. J.H. Clarke talked often about the Pope saving Europe by draining the internecine warfare into the Holy Lands before Europe depopulated itself.

48. Andrew Pollack, "Frugal Koreans Rush to Rescue Their Rapidly Sinking Economy." *The New York Times,* 12/16/97, p. 1.

49. Karen De Witt, "A Culture of Exclusion: In Japan, Blacks As Outsiders." *The New York Times,* 12/10/95, p. 4.

50. Sidney Wilhelm (1971). *Who Needs the Negro?* New York: Anchor Books.

51. Citing Chancellor Williams, *The Destruction of Black Civilization* (Chicago: Third World Press, 1976), we quote from Part I, "What became of the Black people of Sumer? the traveller asked the old man, "for the ancient records show that the people of Sumer were Black. What happened to them? " "Ah," the old man sighed. "They lost their history, so they died. . . . "   — A Sumer Legend

52. Oba T'Shaka (1995). *Return to the African Mother Principle of Male and Female Equality, Volume I.* Oakland, CA: Pan Afrikan Publishers.

★ Special thanks to *Adisa Makalani* for notes references.

Part Two

UNDERSTANDING BLACK ADOLESCENT MALE VIOLENCE

Its Prevention and Remediation

To give up the task of reforming society
is to give up one's responsibility as a free man

–Alan Paton

Introduction

We are all familiar with the crime statistics — the explosively escalating number of homicides among Afrikan American inner-city youth; with the trafficking in cocaine derivatives and their violent, socially devastating side effects on Afrikan American communities across the land; with the virtual reign of terror in our streets perpetuated by relatively small but menacing gangs of youths, muggers, robbers and thieves; with the appalling waste of the "young, gifted and Black."

We will therefore not repeat twice-told tales in this volume. We will however attempt to offer a preliminary outline of some of the most important causes of the phenomena of Black male adolescent criminality. This task was undertaken not in an attempt to "explain away" or rationalize the misbehavior of Black delinquent youths, particularly violent youths, but to provide a causal analysis of Black adolescent criminality which will permit a host of practical solutions to the problems it represents.

In this volume we present what may be called an "interactionist" explanatory approach to understanding the causes of Black male adolescent criminality in many of America's ghettos. Unlike the standard obscurantist, defensive, question-begging, one-factor explanations offered by Eurocentric criminology which predictably ends up blaming the victims — and recommending their lengthy incarceration and/or execution — we offer herein a multi-causal explanation, the implications of which if appropriately translated into educational, rehabilitative, social and institutional reorganization, would move us beyond blaming to resolving.

The resolution of problems of criminality, drug trafficking and abuse, of academic, occupational and social failure of too many Afrikan American inner-city youth while not instigated by the Afrikan American community, must be initiated and executed by that community. While these problems must be borne and ultimately resolved by the whole of the nation, by both White and Black America, it is incumbent on the Afrikan American community, its scholars, leaders and members to arrive at a consensus concerning their causes and to become a unified and effective social-political catalyst for their solution. The text of this volume presents a suggested causal analysis which in no way claims to be complete, totally veridical or definitive but which may help to provide a basis or foundation for construction of theoretical and workable approaches to drastically ameliorating and preventing much of the youthful antisocial and self-defeating, self-destructive behavior which plagues our communities today.

Our thesis is that Black male adolescent criminality is the principal outcome of (1) White-on-Black violence which in its many varied forms, began with the enslavement of Afrikans and has continued unrelentingly to this very moment; (2) the fact that Black male criminality, whether alleged or actual, is a deliberate creation of White American-dominated, race-based society and serves a political, sociopsychological and economically necessary role in maintaining that society[1]; (3) and the unrelenting and the collective ego-defensive and politico-economic needs for White America, to criminalize, denigrate, and degrade Black America.[2]

We further hypothesize that the White American racist need to perceive Black Americans as socially, morally, behaviorally and intellectually inferior, in addition to being innately criminally inclined. Expressed as a continuous and tireless media campaign assault on the character of Afrikan people, history and culture, creates and sustains a false,

1. For a fuller explanation of this proposition and how it is actualized in Black-on-Black violence, please read *Black-on-Black Violence* by the author.

2. Ibid.

misdirected, aversive state of consciousness in the Afrikan American community. This state of consciousness interacting with the negative social and material conditions under which White racism forces Black Americans to live, makes many Afrikan American youth, particularly inner-city, poverty-stricken youth, vulnerable to antisocial behavior. Furthermore, we contend that the ordinary crises common of adolescence, which represent extraordinary crises for Black youths in the ghettos of White America, interact with historical and contemporary White-on-Black violence and racism, and the uniquely negative socioeconomic conditions maintained by the White-dominated racist status quo, to literally drive many Afrikan American male adolescents pell mell into the clutches of criminality.

Our thesis, however, does not rest the case of Black male adolescent criminality at the feet of White American communal perfidy and leave it there while the Black American community helplessly implores the heartless White American political-economic establishment to resolve its especially life-threatening problems not of its own making. For having been thrown into a hole the Afrikan American and Afrikan world communities must climb their way out under their own initiative and power.

We believe that the recommendations we suggest in the relevant section of this volume, if appropriately and vigorously implemented, provide some doable, effective, deterrent and preventative means for dealing with the problems of Black male adolescent criminality and antisocial conduct. It lies within the Provence and power of the Afrikan American community to implement them. The recommendations are by no means exhaustive or fully detailed, merely suggestive. We do not pretend to have the answers. These must be provided by the Afrikan American community itself. We only hope our attempts herein make some contribution to the solution and not to the problem.

Amos N. Wilson

Chapter 1

Origin and Impact of Adolescent Black-on-Black Male Violence

The following discussion provides an outline delineating the major causes of Black-on-Black violence among male adolescents. The scope of the present volume does not permit a fully narrated discussion of the many variables which confluently determine Black-on-Black violence. The outline below is meant to suggest the role the Afrocentric curriculum can possibly play in alleviating the plague of violence which is devastating the lives and futures of large numbers of adolescent Black males and vitiating the viability of many Afrikan American inner-city communities. The continuation and increase of adolescent Black-on-Black violence threaten the ultimate survivability of both the Afrikan American and Pan-Afrikan communities. The psychodynamics of Black-on-Black violence, its politico-economic function in the United States, and the threat it represents to the viability of the Afrikan American community is detailed by the author in another book, *Black-on-Black Violence: The Psychodynamics of Black Self-Annihilation in Service of White Domination.*

White-on-Black Violence

Violence is a form of social interaction, a type of social relationship. It is rooted in social history and represents a type of proaction and reaction relative to that history. Violence occurs in a social-historical-cultural context and cannot be divorced from it. Essentially social in its origins, nature and outcomes, criminality, its rates, prevalences and social locations reflect the socioeconomic, sociopolitical dynamics of the society of which it is a product. Crime and interpersonal violence do not originate and have their being in a societal vacuum. They are therefore genetically rooted in society. A society such as American society which breeds a very broad variety and extraordinary quantity of criminality and violence, whether they characterize the society as a whole or some identifiable segment of it, may arguably and justifiably be referred to as a "crimogenic society," a society which breeds unusual numbers and types of criminals and a relatively high level of crime and violence. Therefore, the origins of Black-on-Black violence in America are rooted in and reflective of the sociocultural, politicoeconomic past and contemporary history of America. Black-on-Black violence speaks not primarily to social relations between Blacks, even though that is of ultimate importance, but to the nature and complexity of the social relations between Whites and Blacks in America and in the world. Black-on-Black violence reflects to a very significant extent the violent origin of America as a nation, the past and contemporary history the violent interactions between White America and Black America. The violence of White America directed toward Black America, both overt and covert, physical and psychological, political and economic, social and cultural, is the violence that begets the largest measurable portion of Black-on-Black violence.

The failure of social scientists to examine Black-on-Black violence and criminality in the context of White-on-Black violence and White criminality in general, has led to the serious misinterpretation of the causes of Black-on-Black violence and Black criminality. It has led to the stereotyping of Blacks, especially young Black males, as innately criminal. There is a need for the dominant elements of White America to maintain their pristine self-image, to perceive themselves as faultless and superior to Afrikans whom they oppress and exploit.

The need by Whites to maintain their highly positive self-perception compels them to deny, distort and rationalize their past criminal and immoral behavior toward Afrikans in America and their current complicity in maintaining the vast majority of Afrikans Americans in conditions of stifling subordination; to project stereotypical images onto Blacks as innately inferior in intellect, character and morals, and on the young Black male as innately crime-prone. Furthermore, this stereotypical perception of Blacks has not only led to "blaming the victims" of White-on-Black violence, but, more importantly, to regressive, social, political, economic, "correctional" and "rehabilitative," educational, social welfare, legislative and administrative policies and practices, which not only have failed to remediate or ameliorate the problems of violence and criminality both within and without the Afrikan American community, but actually have exacerbated them.

EuroAmerican society has an original and unbroken history of violence against its Afrikan inhabitants. This society had its violent origins in the near-decimation of native peoples, the theft of their lands and resources, the enslavement of Afrikan peoples and theft of their dignity, identity, culture, humanity, along with their economic productivity and inalienable right to be free. The physical and psychological violence of White America against Black America which began with Afrikan slavery in America has continued to this moment in a myriad of forms: wage slavery and peonage; economic discrimination and warfare; political-economic disenfranchisement; Jim Crowism; general White hostility and Klan terrorism; lynching; injustice and "legal lynching," the raping of Black women and the killing of Black men by Whites which have gone unredressed by the justice system; the near-condoning and virtual approval of Black-on-Black violence; differential arrests, criminal indictments and incarceration of Whites and Blacks, etc.; segregation; job, business, professional and labor discrimination; negative stereotyping and character assassination; housing discrimination; police brutality; addictive drug importation; poor and inadequate education; inadequate and often absent health care; inadequate family support, etc. This list should make us mindful of the fact that American society is crimogenic, particularly with regard to Afrikan American adolescent and young adult males, not necessarily just because of its criminal and immoral origins — not because of what may be called its "original sins." For original sins can be atoned for, restituted, reparated and forgiven. American society can be described as crimogenic because it *denies* its commission of these sins, and to add insult to injury, attempts to rationalize and justify its sinful behavior toward Afrikan Americans by impugning and slandering their ethnocultural origin and character, blaming them for their socioeconomic, sociopolitical oppression, and by continuing to actively oppose their inherent right to be free, self-defining and self-determining.

Community Effects of Black Male Homicide

According to a report by the Secretary's Task Force on Black Minority Health (1985), homicide is the primary cause of death for Black males between the ages of 15 and 34. The U.S. Department of Justice (1987) reported that in 1986 Blacks accounted for 44 percent of all murder victims. Between 1978 and 1987, the average annual homicide rates for young Black males were 5 to 8 times higher than for young White males; 4 to 5 times higher than for young Black females; and 15 to 22 times higher than for young White females (*The New York Times*, 1990). During this period of time, some 20,315 young males were killed. Some 78 percent of these homicides, 15,781 Black male homicides, involved the use of firearms.

Citing statistics provided from a report on Black male homicide compiled by the Federal Centers for Disease Control (Robert Froehlke, principal author), *The New York Times* (1990) reported that the homicide rate among Black males is "rising fastest among those ages 15 to 19, indicating that violent death [is] becoming increasingly a problem among adolescents." In 1987, homicides among Black males accounted for 42 percent of the deaths of males between ages 15 to 24. Quoting Robert Froehlke of the Federal Centers for Disease Control, *The New York Times* (1990) reported the following information:

> In some areas of the country it is now more likely for a black male between his 15th and 25th birthday to die from homicide than it was for a United States soldier to be killed on a tour of duty in Vietnam.

Citing evidence presented by Rosenberg and Mercy (1986), and Dietz (1987), Bell and Jenkins (1990) indicate that "it has been estimated that for every completed homicide, there are 100 assault victims." Bell and Jenkins further indicate some of the "staggering" emotional and economic costs to the Afrikan American community entailed by Black-on-Black violence and homicide. They include the following results:

- The loss of many men prior to or just entering into their prime years of work and family development.
- The loss of prime productive years by the perpetrators of homicidal acts and the lowering of the social status, marketability and employability of ex-offenders, thereby increasing their chances of continuing their homicidal and violent activity.
- Accelerating the already declining male-female ratio thereby distorting the structural characteristics of the Black family, and impairing its socioemotional and economic health as a consequence.
- Emotional pain and scars which may emotionally skew the lives of the survivors of the victim and the relatives and friends of the perpetrator as well.

- Emotional, behavioral and residual emotional disturbances, e.g., symptoms of post-traumatic stress.

- The emotional and behavioral disturbances and residual emotional scars, e.g., symptoms of post-traumatic
stress experienced by the victim's survivors and in some
instances, disturbances resulting from the witnessing of
violence by children who are relatives, neighbors,
friends of the victim or innocent bystanders who
happen to be children, may contribute to cycles of
family and intragroup violence.

- Random violence serves to maintain a tone of terrorism,
states of chronic stress, suspicion and paranoia in inner-
city communities.

- Fear of and loss of faith in Black youth.

- Isolation and economic disinvestment of the inner-city
communities thereby helping to bolster criminality.

- The institution of a virtual police state, semi-perpetual
martial law and concentration-like camp atmosphere in
many inner-city communities.

- Invasion of schools and other social institutions by
violence or fear of violence.

- Loss of hope, the instigation and maintenance of
personal and social apathy and incipient hostility.

The Psychosocial Aftereffects of White Racism

The list of White people's attacks on Black people is long
and dreary. It is this list of continuing White-on-Black violence
which for the most part breeds the psychological states and
psychological attitudes, relations and behaviors which under
certain circumstances further lead to Black-on-Black violence
in many of its various shades, gradations and forms. Historical
and contemporary forms of White-on-Black racism and
violence induce and maintain in varying degrees the following
psychological states in all Afrikan Americans.

Chronic Anger — ranging from overt, barely controlled, easily-triggered rage to profoundly repressed, over-compensated even-temperedness, passivity and submissiveness.

Chronic Frustration — resulting from being prevented from reaching desired and important goals due to a wide range of obstacles put in place by White-dominated society or from knowing or sensing that their ability to reach desired goals can be arbitrarily inhibited or facilitated by dominant Whites — that their destiny rests inordinately in the hands of Whites. Reactions to frustration may be expressed in a broad variety of ways, e.g., anger; fear; aggressiveness-overt, passive, and/or displaced; apathy (learned helplessness); dependency; regression; depression; fantasy; lowered aspirations; substitute satisfactions; emotional and intellectual insulation.

Chronic Conflict and Ambivalence — Love-hate relations with and attitudes toward Whites are internalized as love-hate conflicts within themselves as individuals and as a community. Chronic conflict and ambivalence also result from the personal, social, political and economic contradictory representations, demands, values, choices, and dilemmas which come with being Black in racist White America.

Displaced Aggression — Provoked to aggressive anger by the White American community and the White American/ European imperialistic establishment, by-and-large, the Afrikan community has contained the expression of its aggressive anger within itself, not directed it at its true sources and causes. This "displaced aggression" expresses itself in many forms in the Black community — horizontal or Black-on-Black violence; various forms of self-depreciation, depreciation of other Blacks, self-defeat, self-narcotization, self-destruction, disruption and/or destruction of the social and physical environment and widespread social rebelliousness, particularly among the youth. Displaced aggression may also be represented as general apathy, indifference and withdrawal or compulsive hedonism.

Internalization of Racist Attitudes — Many in the Afrikan American community having been misinformed, misdirected and miseducated by their White American oppressors and having arrived at the mistaken conclusion that their suffering is caused by their blackness, their being perceived as different by their White oppressors—and not caused by the psycho-pathology of White racism—internalize white racist stereotypes of themselves and attempt to deny their ethnicity by identifying with and/or imitating the behavior and attitudes of their White oppressors. Internalization and imitation are potent sources of Black mutual disrespect, Black internal communal conflict, Black-on-Black violence, Black self-alienation, self-hatred, self-abnegation of various types. They are also potent instigators of class divisions and disunity within the Afrikan American community. This is especially the case when the middle and upper classes of that community are irresistibly attracted toward the way of life of their White oppressor counterparts and share an overpowering aspiration to assimilate with them.

Chronic Sense of Threat, Vulnerability and Anxiety — conditioned by a long history of unprovoked, irrational, egregious White hostility and physical abuse, official abuse (e.g., police brutality), psychological abuse; surrounded by Whites and other ethnic groups who are known to harbor unfriendly, hostile, suspicious attitudes toward them due to their social status in American society; and not knowing under what circumstances these attitudes may be overtly or subtly expressed, induces and maintains a chronic, often unconscious sense of threat, vulnerability and anxiety in Blacks. Threat involves the anticipation of harm, rejection or humiliation— reactions highly associated with white-black social encounters.

Ego-defense Orientation — The unrelenting need to protect against the aversive situations and conditions listed above; to protect against self-devaluation, emotional hurt, loss of confidence, anxiety, physical harm and to meet the contradictory adjustive demands of being Black in White America, tends to stimulate in Afrikan Americans the construction and intense use of ego-defense mechanisms. Defense mechanisms involve the use of fundamentally unconscious processes by which a person defends himself against threat and anxiety by distorting reality or denying the existence of certain relevant aspects of it and by engaging in some form of self-deception.

Compensatory Striving — Related to the ego-defensive orientation described above, this orientation often occurs in Blacks in reaction to feelings of inadequacy, rejection, low status, unattractiveness generated by White racism by disguising, denying or counterbalancing these feelings by intense social climbing, intense striving for social acceptance and prestige, personal over-achievement, striving to identify with their oppressors. Additional compensatory reactions may include the oppressive-compulsive emphasizing of and striving to attain socially desirable or valued traits and the consuming of items in order to cover feelings of inadequacy, social overconformity, extreme religiosity or their opposites, extreme nonconformity and amorality.

Relative Powerlessness and Fatalism — White power advantages and socioeconomic domination, Black power disadvantages and socioeconomic subordination, "perverse White paternalism" and Black dependency, imply too many Blacks that their fate is not in their own hands, but the hands of their White oppressors. The White-Black power differential potently breeds Black fatalistic attitudes toward their situation—the belief that they are powerless or that their power is relatively limited by White authority relative to resolving their problems. Lacking penetrating insight into the very human nature of their White oppressors and the fragility of their system of oppression, deceived by racist propaganda, many, if not most Blacks, harbor an almost mystical belief in the absolute power, invulnerability, invincibility and immortality of their White oppressors.

Consumer Orientedness — Reduced to the socioeconomic role of wage-earners, cheap and surplus labor, "hewers of wood and carriers of water," the only other role position left to Blacks by the White owners of "the means of production" and service organizations is that of consumers. Through mass media manipulation and political propaganda, the need to exhibit social status symbols and to compensate for feelings of inadequacy resulting from social marginality as well as sociological necessity, Blacks too frequently over-consume and come to view consumption as an end in itself.

The consumer-orientedness of Afrikan Americans compounds their problems of unemployment, poverty, the nonexistence or non, or relatively weak, functionality of vital social, economic, political, cultural, educational institutions. This further reduces Black political power and influence and engenders strong tendencies toward political-economic disorganization and social-political economic disunity.

Restricted and Conflicting Affectionate Relations — Having internalized White racist perceptions of themselves, perceptions which lower their self- and social-esteem, very large numbers of Blacks are prone to host various conflicts, distortions and fears regarding affectionate attitudes and relations among themselves. This does not imply that Blacks are incapable of love and affection, and that Blacks do not demonstrate these states and relations. This certainly is not the case. However, it is arguable that these states and relations must be so relatively constricted, tenuous, limited in scope, or conflicted or troubled by their oppressive existence, that they do not gain the unifying sociopolitical and economic potency which would permit the Afrikan American community to collectively overthrow its White American oppressors. Because high levels of love for family and race, high levels of social, political, economic cooperation, reliability, mutual trust and responsibility among Blacks are inimical to the continuity of White domination, White disinformation and negative propaganda, economic machinations must operate "overtime" to vitiate or functionally restrict fully viable Black affectionate and cooperative relations.

Stress — The psychosocial effects of White racism described above combine to produce and maintain chronic levels of conscious and unconscious stress in Black Americans. Depending on a number of other personal and social factors, stress in the Afrikan American community ranges across a spectrum of relatively mild to extremely severe and life-threatening social, psychological and physiological disequilibrium and disease.

Adolescent Crises of Inner-city Youth

To the psychological outcomes of White-on-Black violence listed above, which are pervasively present in Afrikan American society and culture and in individual Afrikan American personalities, must be added the special psychological and subcultural outcomes generated by adolescence, in general, and Black adolescence, in particular. The transitional nature of adolescence is problematic for Afrikan American adolescents particularly as they struggle to define themselves and find their way in the confusing and distracting context of an oppressed, exploited Afrikan American community and a dominant, hostile, racially-oppressive and exploitative European American-dominated society. The forbidding complexity of this situation as represented in the self-perceptions, world-views, attitudes and behaviors of Black adolescents may, in interaction with a number of other personal, valuational, familial, social and economic factors, lead to Black-on-Black violence (including violence against the self).

The factors which characteristically and generally define adolescence in America and which, when represented in the collective personality of Black adolescents, interact with factors related to "being Black in White America," include the following:

- The effort to resolve critical issues concerning self-identity (including ethnic identity), sexual, gender and social identities.
- Efforts to establish and maintain self-esteem (for males — masculinity); efforts to deal with issues revolving around the acceptance and rejection of social norms, adult and parental values and demands, adult authority and control.
- Body image; self-consciousness and self-confidence.
- Emotional liability, i.e., moodiness; boredom; confusion about life, its meaningfulness and purpose and a sense of direction.
- Social acceptance and popularity relative to the peer group.
- General feelings of alienation; anomie; powerlessness; need for attention.
- Vocational and career choices and possibilities.
- Intellectual, cognitive/behavioral development and prowess.
- Issues revolving around status symbols — clothing; hair styles; body adornments; automobiles; money and invidious comparisons of the self with others, race and nationality.

Socioeconomic Context of Inner-city Youth

The critical issues of adolescence as they are uniquely represented in Black adolescents, especially Black male adolescents within the context of the Afrikan American community, encircled as it is and in many ways negatively influenced by the European American community, do not necessarily lead to adolescent Black-on-Black violence. Whether such violence occurs, depends of how the issues of adolescence are dealt with and resolved. However, the methods by which Black adolescents, the resolutions of the crises faced by Black adolescents and the outcomes which flow from them, are heavily influenced by the general psychosocial orientation common to the Afrikan American community which are reflective of that community's experience in America and more important, by the contemporary socioeconomic arena in which Black adolescents carry out their struggle for survival and fulfillment.

The same or similar adolescent concerns and critical issues are coped with and resolved by different means and with different outcomes during different periods of time; depending on different environmental, political, economic, familial, communal, and sociocultural circumstances, class and family backgrounds; religious commitments or ethical/value orientations; levels of income; levels of education; residential location; personal competencies (i.e., "intellectual abilities, social and physical skills and other special abilities" (Atkinson, et al., 1987); long-term expectancies and personal ability to plan and regulate self-behavior. All these factors combine to interact with the foregoing sociohistorical factors, adolescent crises and the factors listed below (the contemporary social-economic context) to determine the negative, or positive, or mixed attitudinal-behavioral outcomes observed in Black adolescents. Where the characteristics just mentioned tend to be inadequate, impaired and generally negative, the attitudinal-behavioral outcomes also tend toward the incompetent, inadequate, maladaptive, illegal, criminal, or violent end of the personal-social spectrum.

Today's Black adolescents, particularly poverty-stricken, un- or under-employed, inadequately educated, alienated Black male adolescents, exist in a socioeconomic, sociopolitical world drastically different from that of their parents, especially of their grandparents. The causes of Black-on-Black adolescent violence can only be garnered from including in a causal equation the interactive relationship between Afrikan sociohistorical relations with White America, their effects as reflected in the collective sociopsychological orientations which characterize the Afrikan American community, the adolescent crises with which Black adolescents must contend, and the contemporary socioeconomic, sociopolitical, sociocultural and ecological contexts within which these crises must be resolved for better or for worse. The contemporary context which surrounds many inner-city Black adolescents includes some of the following characteristics:

- High levels of adult and adolescent unemployment, poverty and overcrowded, inadequate, often unhealthy living conditions.
- Very inadequate preschool, primary and secondary school education; inadequate job-training facilities and preparation.
- An overwhelmingly segregated urban existence.
- A post-modern/industrial/de-industrialized world.
- A world where data and information processing is becoming the basic industry of America in contrast to its factory-based, labor-intensive past where poorly educated, uneducated, unskilled persons and school dropouts could find employment. This catchment or safety net essentially no longer exists.
- A world of television and mass marketing, advertising specifically designed to evoke consummatory desires and artificial needs in adolescents and children.
- A time of rising expectations (with an increasing poverty of means of fulfilling them).
- A time of family dissolution (the characteristic single-headed Black family of current renown began after the 1960s).

- A time of conservative, if not hostile, governments on national and state levels.
- A time of dramatic demographic changes in the American population and changes in the power and economic relations in the world.
- An inner-city world characterized by the absence or dysfunctionality of vital sociocultural, socioeconomic institutions which can deal appropriately with the demands of the 21st century.
- An inner-city world which in many instances resembles a police state or which has been ignored and abandoned to its self-destruction by the government and unconcerned citizens.
- A world of armed, violence-prone, hedonistically oriented, delinquent, criminally inclined gangs and peer groups.
- An urban world flooded by addictive drugs, infectious diseases, firearms of all sizes, types and power.
- An urban, national and international market which provides little room for Black manufacturing, wholesaling, retailing, service or professional activity.

Chapter 2

Sociopathy and Psychopathy

The sociohistorical origins of America, the generally negative sociohistorical and contemporary relations between White and Black America and their pervasive effects on the psychosocial orientations or tendencies and material conditions of Black America, the relative absence or inadequacy of personal/competencies and communal institutions and organizations, the subcultural context we just described, interact to induce in many Black adolescent males a state of consciousness which lends itself to hysteria, impulsivity, dyssocial and sociopath-like behavior. There exists a general tendency for the dominant elements of White America to utilize their power and influence to inculcate these tendencies in Afrikan Americans in order to maintain the effectiveness and efficiency of their dominance. It is in the Black-on-Black violent adolescent that we see so dramatically expressed, the successful inculcation of these tendencies.

In the context of today's Black urban ghettos, Afrikan American youth, unprotected by a firm Afrikan-centered identity and consciousness, unguided by a deep and abiding sense of higher purpose, untutored and untrained by strong, independent Afrikan-centered family and cultural institutions, are prone to fall victim to a series of projective, political and economic assaults on their personalities, perceptions and perspectives which predispose many of them toward a life of crime and violence. These assaults on the psyche of these vulnerable adolescents which are but the aftereffects of the same assaults against the collective psyches of their ethnocultural group, their class, local community and family are such that many react to them with psychopathic- or sociopathic-like tendencies. These, what we may term "psychopathoid" or "sociopathoid" tendencies are less severe and more remediable versions of the classic psychopathic or sociopathic disorders. A series of definitions of these disorders by various authors will give the reader a "feel" for their essential nature and antisocial implications. As cited by Millon (1969), the *sociopathic personality disturbance, antisocial reaction* refers to:

> chronically antisocial individuals who are always in trouble, profiting neither from experience nor punishment, and *maintaining no real loyalties to any person, group, or code.* They are frequently callous and hedonistic, showing marked emotional immaturity, with lack of a sense of responsibility, lack of judgment and *an ability to rationalize this behavior so that it appears warranted, reasonable and justified.* [Emphasis added]

Millon additionally cites McCord and McCord (1964) as describing the psychopath or sociopath in the following manner:

> His conduct often brings him into conflict with society. The psychopath is driven by primitive desires and an exaggerated craving for excitement. In his self-centered search for pleasure, he ignores restrictions of his culture. The psychopath is highly impulsive. He is a man for whom the moment is a segment of time detached from all others. His actions are unplanned and guided by his whims. The psychopath is aggressive. He has learned few socialized ways of coping with frustration. The psychopath feels little, if any, guilt. He can commit the most appalling acts, yet view them without remorse. The psychopath has a warped capacity for love. *His emotional relationships, when they exist are meager, fleeting and designed to satisfy his own desires.* These last two traits, guiltlessness and lovelessness, conspicuously mark the psychopath as different from other men. [Emphasis added]

Gough (1948) describes behavior characterized as antisocial, psychopathic, or sociopathic in the following way:

> [O]verevaluation of immediate goals as opposed to remote or deferred ones, *unconcern over the rights and privileges of others when recognizing them would interfere with personal satisfaction in any way*; impulsive behavior, or apparent incongruity between the strength of the stimulus and the magnitude of the behavioral response; *inability to form deep or persistent attachments to other persons or to identify in interpersonal relationships*; poor judgment and planning in attaining defined goals; apparent lack of anxiety and distress over social maladjustment and unwillingness or inability to consider maladjustment qua maladjustment; *a tendency to project blame onto others and to take no responsibility for failures*; meaningless prevarication, often about trivial matters in situations where detection is inevitable; almost complete lack of dependability of and willingness to assume responsibility; and, finally, emotional poverty.

We italicized portions of above citations to bring attention to those characteristics of sociopathic or "sociopathic" behavior in Black male adolescents which in good part are the result of the White American assault on the collective psyche and material conditions of Afrikan Americans noted at the beginning of this section. This especially refers to results of the projection of negative stereotypes by influential White American media onto Afrikan Americans combined with the other inducible co-factors listed above.

The lack or inadequate knowledge of the tremendously positive sociocultural history of Afrikan peoples, of the testaments to the high intellectual, civil and moral character of peoples of which they are descendants, and the tenuousness, restricted range, or rather low level of self-esteem which reflect these prior conditions, leave many Black adolescents unresistingly open to the internalization of projected negative Afrikan stereotypes and image distortions by the dominant EuroAmerican community. The internalization of negative stereotypes of Afrikan peoples, of themselves, and the internalization of White racist attitudes toward their people and themselves lead to an estrangement, an alienation from themselves as persons and their people as a group.

Internalization of White racist projections onto Afrikan people motivates in many adolescent Black males a conscious and/or unconscious tendency to disavow membership in the Afrikan ethnocultural group; a tendency to "dis-identify" with other Afrikan Americans and — with the exception of family and peers — a tendency to feel a certain amount of contempt, hostility or indifference toward other Afrikan Americans and all things "Black" or Afrikan. These tendencies together operate to effectively destroy or impair any feelings of loyalty to the Afrikan American community, its members, as well as Afrikans the world over. There also may exist no sense of loyalty to the moral codes of the group as well as an actual tendency to directly flaunt or attack such codes. These alienated attitudes and behavioral tendencies predispose some Black adolescents to violently assault other members of the Afrikan American community without a sense of guilt or remorse. As a matter of fact, some may gain a sense of cathartic relief, sense of pleasure or power after having committed an unprovoked assaulted on or having exploited another fellow Afrikan. The tendency to break moral codes, besides possibly reflecting an absence of effective moral training, reflects the fact the violent Black adolescent has witnessed the breaking of such codes without impunity by the larger dominant EuroAmerican community (its ruling classes) while loudly proclaiming its moral superiority to its Afrikan victims. Moreover, these youths have also witnessed the reactive and concomitant breaking of such codes in their family and primary group. The psychological and material gains, the pleasure, power, privileges, prestige and other advantages achieved by the dominant EuroAmerican society and perhaps persons and groups in his community with which he is familiar, through their victimization of Afrikans may serve as potent demonstrations of what is to be gained from the self-serving, self-centered pursuit of one's own satisfactions without regard for the pain to fellow Afrikans such pursuits may cause.

In his perception of the hypocritical behavior of the dominant EuroAmerican community toward the Afrikan-American community — the former abusing and exploiting the latter in every possible way and then blaming the latter community as responsible for its own victimization; rationalizing its anti-Black attitudes and behaviors in terms of defending itself the alleged depredations of the latter community thereby denying any responsibility for its actions — the Black-on-Black violent adolescent may find a model for rationalizing his own psychopathological behavior toward other Afrikans and then blaming them for their own victimization by him.

The reactive internalization of negative EuroAmerican attitudes toward themselves; rationalizing his own pathological behavior in ways imitative of the anti-Black rationalizations of the dominant EuroAmerican group; accepting the self-serving rationalizations of his delinquent peers help, the Black violent adolescent to shape his own rationalizing tendencies, his tendencies to blame his victims, others and circumstances for his own irresponsible behavior.

The Black-on-Black violent adolescent develops his own victimology in order to justify victimizing others, especially his fellow Afrikans. Based on a reactionary, self-serving biased perception of reality, this violent "sociopathoid" adolescent may exhibit one or more of the following characteristics (based on five characteristic features of the sociopathic disorder, developed by McCord and McCord, 1964, as cited in Millon, 1969).

Disdain for Social Conventions   Perceiving the fact that in too many instances racist EuroAmericans, the Euro-American establishment, the authorities, persons and communities which are made to symbolize it act as if the established customs, laws and guidelines which they themselves formulated and approved and which are presented as applying equally to all groups, do not in fact apply to themselves in their relationships to the AfroAmerican community or to any of its constituents, the adolescent sees no reason why he should follow the rules either. This attitude is doubly reinforced when the disdain for social conventions is flaunted by influential role models or peers.

Deceptive Facade　Having intuited that the dominant Euro-American society and its AfroAmerican imitators, "despite their disrespect for the rights of others, . . .present a social mask, not only of civility but of sincerity and maturity" (Millon, 1969), the criminal or violent Black adolescent sees no good reason why he should not "con" and manipulate his fellow Afrikans order to reap the same benefits as those he has chosen to imitate.

Inability or Unwillingness to "Adjust" Following Punishment. Millon (1969) intimates that "many sociopaths are of better than average intelligence, exhibiting both clarity and logic in their cognitive capacities. Yet they display a marked deficiency in self-insight, and rarely exhibit. . . foresight [regarding] the implications of their behavior. The habits and needs to abuse and exploit Afrikans are so deeply rooted in the EuroAmerican psyche, that the racist attitudes and behaviors toward Afrikan Americans on the part of Euro-Americans are relatively impervious to reasoning, moral suasion, demonstrations and punitive reactions on the part of the AfroAmerican community. Such actions on the part of the latter community are themselves deemed by the Euro-American community as unreasonable, unfair, intimidating and intended to do harm to or victimize it. The criminal, violent Black adolescent uses the same or similar effective technique to feign innocent victimization by those he victimizes and thereby establishes a new "justification" for continuing his irresponsible attitudes and behaviors. This scenario may also be paralleled within the context of the adolescent's own socially reactionary primary group.

Impulsive Hedonism   Witnessing the single-minded pursuit of treasure, pleasure, adventure, power and advantage by EuroAmericans (as presented in their myths, legends, media productions and history books as well as daily life), their acting as if they were immune from danger; misperceiving the short-sighted, foolhardy behavior of members of his primary group, the criminal or violent adolescent likewise perceives this approach as "idea" for handling his low tolerance for frustration, delay of gratification, boredom, and for providing himself with one exciting and momentarily gratifying escapade after another. This especially applies when his access to such sources of gratification is owned or blocked by persons for whom he has little or no respect, for whom he feels contempt, who are perceived by him as undeserving and/or weak or vulnerable.

Insensitivity or Disregard for the Feelings of Others   The seeming incapacity for EuroAmericans, particularly their political leaders and representatives, to share tender feelings, to experience genuine affection and love for another [especially outside their ethnocultural group, i.e., AfroAmericans] or to empathize with the needs and distress of others—the seeming pleasure many EuroAmericans appear to gain in the thought and process of hurting others [e.g., AfroAmericans]; in seeing them downtrodden and suffering pain and misery; often go out of their way to exploit others; and yet not be punished or otherwise chastised or penalized for the distress and pain they leave in their wake but seem to enjoy all the more the tangible fruits of their cunning and deceit; to see the fruits even multiply—leaves an almost indelible impression on the would-be criminal Black adolescent. When these examples set by the larger, dominant EuroAmerican society are successfully duplicated by the adolescent's neighborhood role models it becomes exceeding difficult to convince him that insensitivity or disregard for the feelings of others does not provide its own abundant and readily available rewards, that crime does not pay.

The victimology of the sociopathoid individual, i.e., his rationale for perceiving himself as victim rather than a perpetrator or victimizer, is based on his restricted and rather paranoid perception of himself as being victimized by others who themselves exhibit a disdain for social conventions; engage in deceptive and hypocritical practices; seem to act without compunction and to perceive any penalties levied against them for even the most obvious or egregious misconduct towards others, as unfair and as a basis for continuing the misbehavior or as a basis for revenge; who evidence a single-minded pursuit of pleasure or needs satisfaction without regard for the painful effects such pursuit may have on others — while forbidding him the same privileges and rights. Thus, the sociopathoid personality is motivated by a deep and abiding sense of and sensitivity to real or perceived unfairness or injustice to obtain his due by any manipulative means necessary. He is an aggrieved person. His grievances whether alleged or actual or some one-sided, exaggerated combination thereof, provide the foundation for his intentional, insensitive abuse and exploitation of others, for his suspension of the Golden Rule.

The reader must note that we are not referring to violent Black adolescent males as psychopaths or sociopaths. We have attempted to demonstrate here how intergroup relations, e.g., between EuroAmericans and AfroAmericans, where one group possesses inordinate power compared to the other and the more powerful group, project negative stereotypes on the weaker, often dependent group, directs overtly and covertly hostile attitudes and behaviors toward the weaker group, and abuses its power over the latter group — may under certain conditions induce attitudinal and behavioral orientations in members of the subordinate group which to a limited degree resemble some of those exhibited by extreme or "classic" psychopaths or sociopaths.

The "classical" or typical sociopath is a deeply and pervasively disturbed personality who generally "tends to be a "loner," with no genuine loyalty to anyone or anything, lacking the power to share and feel affection toward ... others [whose] behaviors are often foolish or purposely aggressive, enacted without apparent rhyme or reason" (Millon, 1969). The behavioral orientation we have labeled "sociopathoid" which while sharing the sociopath's disdain for social conventions along with a number of the other sociopathic characteristics pointed out above is more similar to "dyssocial reactions" which, according to Millon "are stimulus-specific responses to circumscribed conditions, usually ... learned as a consequence of faulty past experiences, these experiences did not permeate the entire fabric of the individual's personality make-up." Millon goes on to indicate that "dyssocial reactions are seen most commonly in group delinquency behaviors and in planned criminal activities." Our "psychopathoid" or "sociopathoid" reaction while certainly not as intensely psychopathically severe and pervasive as the psychopathic or sociopathic reaction, is significantly less benign than is the dyssocial reaction.

Sociopathoid behavior is the product of painful experiences resulting from rather specific types of familial-primary group relations, inadequate socialization experiences inside and outside the home (schools and other cultural institutions), occurring during early childhood and the witnessing, observation, or intuitive understanding of how the abuse of power, cunning, misuse of advantage and opportunity, deception and the single-minded, insensitive pursuit of self-centered goals and ambitions, can be utilized to attain both highly desired material and nonmaterial rewards which under any other circumstances would apparently not be available. The reactions to painful, distorted social relations and inadequate socialization experiences, to the witnessing or imagining of the one-sided abuse of advantage for selfish gain, manifest such *mis*perceived traumatic potential that the sociopathoid individual finds it necessary to reject his real self; to repress empathetic identity with his ethnocultural group, pledge allegiance to its "flag"; to repress normal human sensitivities and normal conscience; and to alienate or estrange himself from the more humane and sensitive inner core of his personality, for fear that if he were to claim his true self and ethnocultural identity — to lift his repressions and come into contact with his true feelings — he would suffer psychological and possibly physical impoverishment, vulnerability, disorganization, or annihilation. Yet it must be kept in mind that the central causal nexus of psychopathoid or sociopathoid reaction or disorders in low-socioeconomic class, inner city Black males is the alienation from their Afrikan identity, consciousness and self and the alienation from an Afrikan-centered community (which they have in common with all other Afrikan American classes) and society in general, brought on by unrelenting, vicious, full variety of assaults against his Afrikan heritage, community and people by hostile and self-serving White imperialist ruling and managing classes.

Black-on-Black violence is by far most likely to occur when alienation of many inner-city males combines with impulsive (i.e., short-sighted, labile, volatile), hysterical (i.e., impressionistic, diffused, distractible) and dyssocial (i.e., peer and/or gang-oriented, *manifestly bent-on disregarding accepted social and moral codes*) orientations which are stimulated and reinforced by the socioeconomic conditions under which they live. Yet we must be ever mindful of the fact that this type of alienation and these maladaptive orientations along with the psychosocial conditions which synergistically conspire to coalesce them into aggressively self-destructive and socially destructive forces, are themselves sociopolitically and socioeconomically instigated and maintained by a self-serving, self-centered upper and ruling class regime. However, such a regime can only hold sway over Afrikan Americans and Afrikans in general as long as their consciousness and identity are not Afrikan-centered.

Chapter 3

Black Adolescent Masculinity
and Antisocial Behavior

While lack of space will not allow us to cover this important matter sufficiently, we must mention that a goodly portion of Black male violence against other Black males is the consequence of unresolved conflicts around masculinity. The resolution of what it means to be a man is a major crisis of adolescence and young adulthood under normal circumstances, how much more the case for the Black adolescent and young adult male under conditions of oppression.

It is well known that the males of a captive or oppressed people are the targets for special and more intense oppression by their captors and oppressors than are their oppressed female counterparts. This is the case simply because their principal captors and oppressors, usually males themselves, expect greater and more nakedly aggressive resistance to their dominance from captive and oppressed males. While not denigrating the resistance and revolutionary roles played by women under oppression, we think that the psycho-historical record will reveal that the freedoms, movements, social assemblies and activities of oppressed males which may be perceived by their oppressors as possibly empowering their abilities to resist and overthrow their masters, are subject to acute surveillance and repression. As an important part of protecting themselves against overthrow and maintaining the effectiveness of their physical, psychological and socio-

104

economic security and dominance, maintaining high levels of masculine self-esteem, self-concept and self-confidence, oppressive males attempt to undermine the physical, psychological and socioeconomic stability and security of oppressed males. Moreover, they undermine and destabilize the masculinity of oppressed males by minimizing their self-esteem, negating and destroying their self-concept, self-perception, their self-confidence, or by severely restricting the development and expression of these factors in ways which would liberate them from their oppression. In a word, the oppressed male is ideally made and kept "nonthreatening" to the oppressive regime of his oppressive male counterpart. The relationship which we have sketched, despite appearances to the contrary, is fairly descriptive at this juncture of the relationship between the oppressive EuroAmerican male and the oppressed Afrikan male in the world today, extending back some several centuries in the past.

In spite of their oppressive conditions Afrikan American males have sought to develop a masculine ideal, a cultural model of what it means to be a man. The approximation of this ideal under the aegis of the oppressive White male regime by the vast majority of Afrikan American males has been remarkable. From their oppressed ranks have emerged generation after generation, from the time of their very captivity in Afrika and enslavement in the New World to this very moment, men who have risen to challenge their oppressors and helped to push back the frontiers of oppression. There have been others who under the most discouraging of circumstances have fed and protected their families and communities and who have contributed their genius to expanding the material, civil and cultural development and prosperity of their people.

Yet there also has been and is too large a minority of Afrikan American males whose immaturity; whose reactionary frustration to the restrictions placed on their masculine possibilities and to the obstacles placed in the way of achieving what they had been told represents the achievement of masculinity; whose training for positive manhood is non-existent or inadequate; whose avoidance of masculine responsibility or confusion about what it means to be a man under oppression, have moved them to accept an incomplete, distorted, self-defeating and, sometimes, self-destructive definition and expression of masculinity. These males, often misguidedly and ignorantly assuming that they are successfully defying White male authority and dominance, defying "the system," expressing their independence and "masculine prerogatives," expressing their "manhood," have been misled or misdirected into violently attacking and corrosively undermining the peace, stability, and the very viability of the Afrikan American community. These males have been provoked by their oppressive circumstances into what we may call a "reactionary masculinity" whose presence and expression are essentially detrimental to the Afrikan American community and, ironically, to their own well-being.

Characteristics of Reactionary Masculinity

- Lacks a sense of social responsibility or social interest.
- Lacks a deep and abiding Afrikan identity and consciousness; exhibits an impoverished empathy for others.
- Tends toward rigid and excessive self-interest, self-centeredness, self-service, intolerance, stubbornness.
- Tends to be opinionated and to view every social encounter as a test to his masculinity, as a struggle for power.
- Mistakenly identifies physicality, crudeness, with masculinity; views domination, insensitivity, unconcern, willingness to injure or kill, seek revenge, as essentially masculine traits.
- Motivated primarily by fear, avoidance, escape, retreat from responsibility, ego-defense, and reactionary frustration; by a deep and ever-present sense of inade-

quacy; by an inferiority complex; and an obsessive need to appear superior.

- Perceives cooperation with other males, submitting to the rightful authority of other males; conceding "points" to other males and relating to them, as humiliating insults to their masculinity.

- Believes the mastery of knowledge, crafts, academic subject-matter, professional expertise, the actualization of intellectual potential, to be essentially feminine.

- Is a conspicuous consumer; consumer-oriented — concerned mainly with parasitically exploiting others, works merely to earn "spending money," i.e., money to spend irresponsibly; is "into" flashy clothes, cars, fads, and styles of all types.

- Motivated and defined by self-alienation; exhibits an absence of self-knowledge; ignorance of his ethnic-heritage; unbounded hedonism; narcissistic drives; deep insecurities regarding the reality of his masculinity and of his masculine courage.

- Lacks self-control, discipline, persistence, and high frustration tolerance; lacks long-term goals and commitment to prosocial values.

Note: The following list of characteristics is derived and quoted from Adler, in Ansbacher & Ansbacher (1956)

- Typified by defensive and compensatory intent, impudence, courage, impertinence, inclination toward rebellion, stubbornness, and defiance, accompanied by phantasies and wishes of the role of a hero, warrior, robber, in short, ideas of grandeur and sadistic impulses. The inferiority feeling finally culminates in a never-ceasing, always exaggerated feeling of being slighted. . . .

- They are attacked much more by the difficulties of life and feel and live as though they were in enemy country. . . . They are therefore selfish, inconsiderate, lacking in social interest, courage, and self-confidence because they fear defeat more that they desire success.

- They consider other people enemies. Later in life they are not adapted for occupation, love, marriage, because they consider only their own welfare and are not looking for the interests of others. Sometimes they turn toward crime, and they are, in childhood, the majority of the problem children.

- They feel curtailed and behave like enemies. They use their strength only if they are stronger, sometimes in a cruel manner against weaker persons or animals. . . . It is difficult to win them and to develop social interest and courage to do useful work.

- For the safeguarding of [their] picture of the world and for the defense of [their] vanity, [they erect] a wall against the demands of actual community life. Without clearly realizing it [themselves], they exclude or shove aside all disturbing problems of life, while they abandon [themselves] utterly to their feelings and to the observation of [their] symptoms.

- They see everything with the eyes of [their] vanity. They approach every situation and problem of life with fearful anticipation as to whether [their] prestige will be assured. . . .

- If [their] vanity is offended, [they] react with cold disdain, marked ill-humor, or downright aggression [Reich, 1970].

- The meaning [they] give to life is a private meaning. No one else is benefitted by the achievement of [their] aims, and [their] interest stops short at [their] own person. [Their] goal of success is a goal of personal superiority, and [their] triumphs have meaning only to themselves . . . . A private meaning is, in fact, no meaning at all.

- [When a criminal they] . . . always look for excuses and justifications, for extenuating circumstances, and for reasons that "force" them to be criminal.

- [Their criminality] is a coward's imitation of heroism. Criminals think they are courageous; but we should not be fooled into thinking the same. *All criminals are actually cowards. They are evading problems they do not feel strong enough to solve. . . . He feels himself incapable of normal success. . . . He hides his feelings of inadequacy by developing a cheap superiority complex.* [Emphasis added]

- [They] regard the partner in love merely as a piece of property, and very often [they] thinks that love can be bought. It is something [they] ought to possess, not a partnership in life. [**Note:** End of quotes from Adler].

- They exhibit essentially what is referred to in psycho-analytic theory as a "phallic character" or "phallic-narcissistic character." Phallic characters are persons whose behavior is reckless, resolute and self-assured — traits, however, that have a reactive character. They reflect a fixation at the phallic level, with an overvalu-ation of the penis and confusion of the penis with the entire body. This fixation is due either to a castration fear [i.e., a fear of failure as a man, fear not being a "real man", fear of having his "manhood" destroyed] . . .or to a defense against temptations, toward an anal-receptive aggression" [i.e., fear of being forced to submit utterly, of falling completely under the power of another, of being made a symbolic passive, homosexual by another man or a "sucker" by a woman] (Fenichel, 1945).

- They measure their manhood by the number of sexual conquests they achieve and the number of children they have sired (in contrast to the number for whom they have assumed paternal responsibility and economic support). They thereby exploit both women and children and help to disfigure and maladapt the family structure, impoverish women, children and communities, and contribute to social dysfunctionality in various forms, including criminalization of the next generation of males.

• They find no deep satisfaction on any level of activity and are forced into continued pursuit and conquest (Lowen, 1958). Therefore, their relationship with women tends to be exploitative, fleeting, unstable, disloyal and unreliable.

• Unconsciously, the penis, in the case of the male of this type, serves less as an instrument of love than as an instrument of aggression, wreaking revenge upon the woman. . . . In the case of the male representatives of this type, the mother is very often the stricter parent, or the father died at an early age or was not married to the mother and was never present (Reich, 1972).

• In their marital relationships they do not "question the belief that the man should always be strong and superior and that the woman should be weak and in need of leadership." The role of the wife is to confirm his masculinity and success (Willi, 1982). This demand in the face of their obvious subordination and failure to achieve true independence when perceived consciously or unconsciously by their partner operate to destabilize or sabotage their relationship or to maintain the relationship in terms of collusive deception and mutual false consciousness.   □

Again we wish to notify the reader that the above-listed characteristics do *not* characterize the large majority of Black males. These traits are most likely to take root and grow in the psyches of young Afrikan American males when they are compelled to live within the "socioeconomic context of inner-city youth" described earlier, and when they are not countered or neutralized by positive family conditions, effective cultural and educational institutions, positive personal-social experiences and relations, and personal competencies. In the absence or inadequacies of the requisite experiences, knowledge, competencies, values and perspectives provided by family, social relations, community and cultural institutions, these males have in common personal constructs of masculinity, implicit theories of what it means to be a man, and concepts of masculine prerogatives whose concrete expression under conducive conditions may lead to academic underachievement, scholastic misconduct, truancy, dropping-out, apathy, vocationally/occupational inadequacy, maladaptive male-female relations, criminality, orientations toward violence, substance abuse and addictions of various types.

However, in the instances of Black adolescent and young adult male delinquency, criminality, and violence masculine immaturity, misperceptions of what it means to be a male or a man, ill-formed definitions and anti-social expressions of masculinity are readily apparent and rather dramatic. This may also be the case in regard to male-female relations, marital and family relations as well. But this does not at all imply that the models of manhood and masculinity demonstrated by law-abiding, fully employed, better educated, trained or skilled, family-oriented and even moral/ethically astute Afrikan American males and men are complete and maturely adaptive. The successful struggles by Black males to maintain the stability of the Black family and community, to advance Afrikan American civil rights and civil liberties, political and economic enfranchisement, educational and occupational interests within the context and confines of White male dominance and racism are to be commended. Within the context and confines of White male dominance and racism however, the failure of "mature" Afrikan American males to assume full responsibility for educating and training Afrikan

American boys and adolescents for productive manhood—their failure to take economic and political control of their national communities; to aggressively move in and capture economic territory, real estate, health and other economic institutions in the larger society and the world so as to alleviate and prevent the conditions of which we speak in this volume; their failure to learn of the realities of power and of power relations between groups and nations; to prepare for the defense of Afrikan peoples against their current and future enemies; their willingness to continue their dependence on the largesse of White males; to submit to the dominance of White males in America and the world; their apparent inability, lack of will or courage to form a nation-within-a-nation and to set as one of their ultimate goals the collapse of White male power advantages; their relative powerlessness to transform the social and economic misfortunes of the Afrikan American community and of the Pan-Afrikan community—glaringly reveal their inadequate preparation for assuming the responsibilities of Afrikan manhood, whether they may be classified prosocial or antisocial, responsible or irresponsible.

The fate of a man, his job, social status, civil rights and liberties, and his family is ultimately tied to the fate of some social group or groups to which he relates. These things can only have meaning and be supported by and within some group context. Personal achievements, in the final analysis, are not individual achievements—but group achievements. Therefore, the preservation of the group, of the fundamental society, is synonymous to preservation of the self. Individual Afrikan males, free-standing Afrikan families and isolated Afrikan communities cannot idly stand by and watch the Afrikan American masses and Afrikan world communities suffer and perish without themselves also encountering the same fate. For those who either through benign neglect or malignant concern would destroy the so-called Afrikan American "underclasses" and the "underdeveloped" Afrikan nations principally because they are Afrikan in ethnic composition or because of their relative defenselessness, would not ultimately hesitate to devour the remaining Afrikan working, middle and working classes and the "developing" Afrikan nations if it were in their interest to do so, and for the very same reasons they devoured the other Afrikan classes and nations. The prevention of these very realistic, possible and ominous eventualities, or to speak more positively, the possibilities for the Pan-Afrikan community to achieve high levels of self-actualization — of realizing its humanistic potentialities and contributing significantly to the true civilizing of America and the world — are intimately related to how the collective Afrikan male defines for himself, what it means to be an Afrikan man in today's world, and how he trains and prepares himself and his sons to realize that definition. Obviously, maleness and manhood are not synonymous. Neither are male adulthood and manhood. Within a cultured context manhood is a conferred status, a socially defined and achieved status. It must be *earned*. Manhood, therefore, involves more than biological maturity, but also includes a special set of social attitudes, behavioral orientations and expressions.

A man's self-definition is always, on some level, a social definition. A man lives, and if necessary, dies for his fundamental ethnic or cultural group. Preparations for achieving manhood status may be very formal in traditional societies or informal or rather subtle and somewhat amorphous as in many modern societies. But even in the latter there exist some types of *rites of passage*, milestones, accomplishments or markers, attitudes and behaviors which are generally perceived as masculine and whose existence and expression are seen as necessary to personal and social well-being and stability.

Gilmore (1990) in a cross-cultural study of manhood provides a number of general characteristics and expectations regarding manhood. Some of the conclusions he reached are quoted below.

Cross-Cultural Concepts and
Expectations Regarding Manhood

- Regardless of other normative distinctions made, all societies distinguish between male and female; all societies also provide institutionalized sex-appropriate roles for adult men and women.

- . . . manhood ideals make an indispensable contribution both to the continuity of social systems and to the psychological integration of men into their community . . . as part of the existential "problem of order" that all societies must solve by encouraging people to act in certain ways, ways that facilitate both individual development and group adaptation. Gender roles represent one of these problem-solving behaviors.

- . . . the manhood ideal is not purely psychogenetic in origin but also a culturally imposed ideal to which men must conform whether or not they find it psychologically congenial. That is, it is not simply a reflection of individual psychology but a part of public culture, a collective representation.

- . . . there is a constantly recurring notion that real manhood is different from simple anatomical maleness, that it is not a natural condition but rather is a precarious or artificial state that boys must win against powerful odds. This recurrent notion that manhood is problematic, a critical threshold that boys must pass through testing, is found at all levels of sociocultural development regardless of what other alternative roles are recognized.

- The data show a strong connection between social organization and production and the intensity of the male image. That is, manhood ideologies are adaptions to social or psychic fantasies writ large. The harsher the environment and the scarcer the resources, the more manhood is stressed as inspiration and goal. This correlation. . .does indicate a systematic relationship in which gender ideology reflects the material conditions of life.

• Because of the universal urge to flee from danger, we may regard "real" manhood as an inducement for high performance in the social struggle for scarce resources, a code of conduct that advances collective interests by overcoming inner inhibitions.

• For [many cultures, e.g.,] the Masai [and] the Samburu [both East Afrikan tribes], the idea of manhood contains the idea of the tribe, an idea grounded in moral courage based on commitment to collective goals. Their construction of manhood encompasses not only physical strength or bravery but also a moral beauty construed as selfless devotion to national identity.

• Again and again we find that "real" men are those who give more than they take; they serve others. Real men are generous, even to a fault. . . .Non-men are often those stigmatized as stingy and unproductive. Manhood therefore is also a nurturing concept, if we define that term as giving, subverting, or other-directed.

• But surprisingly, "real" men nurture, too, although they would perhaps not be pleased to hear it put this way. Their support is indirect and thus less easy to conceptualize. Men nurture their society by shedding of their blood, their sweat, and their semen, by bringing home food for both child and mother, by producing children, and by dying if necessary in faraway places to provide a safe haven for their people.   □

Cross-cultural studies of manhood indicate that what it means to be a man in a particular culture is derived from the recurrent or ongoing problems of living faced by that culture, the modes of production, social activities and relations perceived as vital for maintaining its integrity and cohesion, and the demands placed on its well-being by external factors and groups. The methods by which boys are trained for manhood, the values extolled as masculine and the cognitive/behavioral characteristics expected of a man, are intimately related to the problems just mentioned.

If the social definition of manhood arrived at and the methods of manhood training do not adequately prepare the males to solve or successfully cope with these problems then their masculinity and its expression will tend to be maladaptive, antisocial and will place the society in serious jeopardy.

In light of the problems of living which must be resolved or controlled by Afrikan American males, e.g., unemployment, underemployment, educational underachievement and inadequacy, male-female and marital-family difficulties, crime, violence, incarceration, and subordination to White male dominance, it should be apparent that there is an urgent need for Afrikan American males and the Afrikan American community to critically reassess, redefine and reconstruct what it means to be an Afrikan man in America and the world today. This new definition of Afrikan manhood must not only be a reactionary one, i.e., based solely on the problems which must be resolved by Afrikan males, but must also be a proactive one, one based on the very positive contributions Afrikan males can make to the community and the world. The new definition cannot be an imitation of their White male counterparts. This is the worst example or model of manhood. In fact, as detailed in Wilson's book, *Black-on-Black Violence*, it is due to the fact that many Afrikan American males internalize the racist attitudes, the egregious and rapacious economic philosophy and approaches, and behavioral orientations of White

American and imperialistic European males which account in good part for the high rates of criminality and intragroup homicide and violence in the Afrikan American community.

Moreover, the frustrations of their not being allowed to play the full "masculine role" in their homes and communities, and the racist restrictions placed on their exercise of the same "masculine prerogatives, privileges and powers permitted White American males—facilitate the induction of mal-adaptive and antisocial behavior in many Afrikan American male youths and adults.

The definition of what it means to be an Afrikan American male must be firmly based on an objective and deep knowl-edge of the sociohistorical experiences of Afrikan peoples; the psychohistorical relations between Afrikans and non-Afrikans, especially Europeans and White Americans; an unflinching analysis of contemporary social, economic, political, cultural, technological and military realities; and realistic projections regarding what the future holds for how that future may be transformed in the interests of Afrikan peoples.

Chapter 4

The All-Male Program or School

To unwittingly imitate one's enemies, to indiscriminately imitate their attitudes and oppressive behaviors; to fail to model one's attitudes and oppressive s to fit one's own circumstances and expectations, is self-defeating and self-oppressing. These are the general outcomes for Afrikan Americans who attend "standard" American schools, establishments designed and managed by their oppressors. The "standard" American school wherein they are unwittingly, indiscriminately prodded to imitate their oppressors, even if "successful" in such institutions, is ill-fitted to their history of oppression and to prepare them for liberation from it. The subjection of the Afrikan American male, who is the special target of hostile White male dominance, to "standard" American education, a major instrument of EuroAmerican socioeconomic supremacy, is tantamount to the genocidal subjection, through him, of the Afrikan American and Pan-Afrikan communities.

Consequently, in recognizing the special problems plaguing the Afrikan American male and the Afrikan American and Pan-Afrikan communities and the failure and inability of American schools as currently designed to resolve or even moderately ameliorate these problems, there has arisen in tandem with the general Afrocentric movement, a movement to design and execute a curriculum exclusively for Afrikan American males. Such a curriculum may be practiced as a special program for males within current coeducational establishments or in separate all-male academies or institutions. Proponents of the all-male programs or institutions argue that the critical situation confronted by Black males and the special needs of these males can best be addressed by special programs or schools.

A number of Afrikan American all-male institutions and programs have already been developed or are in the process of development. The programs may include all-male classes taught by Afrikan American male instructors which stress Afrikan cultural heritage and history. The male instructors serve as role models and are expected to exhibit an empathic understanding of their male students and an ability to cope more successfully with the cognitive-behavioral, attitudinal-emotional problems some of these students may present. These programs also emphasize the teaching of positive values, linking the learning experience to real life problems, the provision of so-called remedial instruction, but more importantly, the provision of a broader and more advanced variety of academic, science and technological subject matter and training classes.

In addition to the cultural-historical, academic-technological, values-oriented emphases, a number of programs and institutions emphasize instructional approaches which are designed to counter specific psychological and psychosocial orientations which are common to Afrikan American students of both genders but which obtain more special and more destructive outcomes when acted-out by males. The approaches also seek to appropriately correct or prevent the development of the maladaptive psychosocial characteristics of the "reactionary masculinity" listed earlier.

The tradition of exclusive male education and training is an ancient and honored tradition in Afrikan societies. This tradition, supported by Afrikan females (who also have the tradition of exclusive female education and training) begins with the recognition as stated by Gilmore that "manhood ideals make an indispensable contribution both to the continuity of social systems and the psychological integration of men into their community." The recognition of the integrative importance of the social institutions of manhood training and masculine ideals is concretely expressed by the practice transitional *rites of passage* or transitional rites found in numerous cultures.

These rites refer to more than symbolic rituals and acts performed to mark changes in social relations and processes. For example, in the case of males or females or other social categories these rites may symbolize and certify the completion of certain special training and preparation to undertake a new social role and function. In the case of the male, these rites may socially signify the completion of some level of training for full manhood or adulthood. "Many *rites de passage* explicitly aim at effecting in individuals certain changes in motivation, appropriate to the newly assumed social roles that are publicly proclaimed by the ritual" (Wallace, 1970). The training, experiential exercises and rituals have the marked advantage of clearly indicating to the individual the end of a particular era in his life and the beginning of a new one and the role expectations and privileges attached to the new role. The absence or ambiguity of such demarcations in the lives of certain individuals or groups may under certain circumstances lead to ambiguities of social identity and social status, to social role confusion and conflicts, social and psychological immaturity, sex role diffusion, irresponsibility, reactive masculinity and antisocial behavior.

Even though post-industrial American society does not explicitly emphasize manhood training and *rites of passage*, there still remains certain experiences, social and occupational milestones which are utilized to mark important transitions in social status and role expectations, such as between boyhood and adolescence, adolescence and young adulthood and full adult maturity and old age. With regard to adolescence and young adulthood some of these points of social demarcation may include completion of high school; accomplishment in sports; acquisition of a valued or prestigious skill, of steady employment; certificates of various types; self-support; entry into and completion of service in the Armed Forces; marriage and parentage; religious conversion; a period of delinquency or rebellion followed by "settling down"; achieving voting age, drinking age and legal adulthood; acceptance of some responsible social position, job, or position of community leadership. Perhaps high school graduation, entry into post-secondary education or training—the acquisition of trade, semiprofessional or professional skills, substantial wage earnings; the ability to be self-supporting or to contribute significantly to family income, marriage and family—still represent certain informal experiences and *rites of passage* which help to define manhood and adulthood and their related role expectations in America today. There exist many other more subtle experiences in and out of school which convey to males expectations regarding masculinity and manhood.

When we examine the points of demarcation indicative of transitions from adolescence to adulthood just mentioned, such as high school graduation, the acquisition of valued employment skills and substantial wage earnings, etc., it is apparent that the failure of many inner-city males to achieve these goals within the expected period of time may lead to one or more of the negative or problematic outcomes centered around definitions of masculinity and manhood.

The degree to which an Afrikan American all-male program and curriculum can provide the intellectual and skills development, occupational preparation, personal and social skills development, moral/ethical and cultural training, sense of meaning and purpose, and positive affirmations of masculinity as well as increase the probability of graduation, Afrikan American males will play a major role in the reformation of the Afrikan American community.

It must be kept in mind that traditional manhood training in Afrikan societies was not only concerned with the mastery of stereotypical manhood skills, especially of warfare and economic modes of production, but also involved training for full participation in the society as adults at all relevant levels of social activity, such as training in the skills of "husbandhood," male-female relations, family-hood, and social responsibility. It also involved the mastery of valued intellectual knowledge, personal and social cooperative and leadership skills. Therefore, the mere separation of males for periods of training and education does not in and of itself imply a training and education of males for chauvinistic and dominant or superior attitudes toward females. As a matter of fact, these separate sessions or periods can be utilized to emphasize those very values, skills and attitudes which evoke a high regard and respect for females, family and community. It is quite apparent at this juncture that the type of co-educational experiences many Afrikan American males have undergone has not and is not achieving these and other desirable and necessary ends.

Many Afrikan American all-male programs or institutions which are in operation or proposed for implementation or institutionalization are centered around the academic and social realization of the Seven Principles of Kwanzaa (the *Nguzo Saba*):

- *Umoja* — Unity
- *Kujichagulia* — Self-determination
- *Ujima* — Collective work and Responsibility
- *Ujamaa* — Cooperative Economics
- *Nia* — Purpose
- *Kuumba* — Creativity
- *Imani* — Faith

As with the multicultural and the Afrocentric curricula, the recency of the development and implementation of Afrikan

American all-male programs and institutions does not allow the presentation of statistical and other formal evaluations of their educational outcomes. However, according Spencer Holland (*Daily News*, Feb. 3, 1991), director of the Center for Educating Afrikan American Males, in the School of Education and Urban Studies of Morgan State University:

> The evidence concerning academic achievement, as well as attendance and behavior, from the Baltimore City Public Schools' demonstration classes at the first, third and sixth grade levels of all boys, taught by men, is very encouraging. Preliminary data show that boys in these classes appear to be faring much better, academically and behaviorally, than their peers from the same communities who are in coed classes.
>
> Evidence from a newly published book, "*Girls & Boys In School: Together or Separate?*," by Cornelius Riordan (Teachers College Press, 1990) which studied the academic achievement of inner-city African American and Latino students in mixed-sex and same-sex Catholic schools, found that both boys and girls in same-sex schools scored significantly higher on standardized achievement tests than African American and Latino boys and girls in mixed-sex schools.

It is important that Afrikan-centered programs for Afrikan Americans boys begin as early as possible. The negative interracial dynamics between Black and White America in general, and more specifically, the embittered clashes between Black and White males, are highly reflected in the dysfunctional psychological and structural dynamics of the Afrikan American family. These dynamics as they are played out in the Black ghettos of America are often acted out in the aggressive and antisocial attitudes and behaviors of Afrikan American boys as early as the preschool years. Such behavior during this boyhood period is highly predictive of scholastic failure and serious delinquent and criminal behavior during the pre-adolescent, adolescent and young adulthood years.

As cited by Wilson and Herrnstein (1985), Conger and Miller (1966) concluded from a longitudinal study of male delinquency which included an analysis of third-grade school records that:

> By the end of third grade, future delinquents were already seen by their teachers as more poorly adapted than their classmates. They appeared to have less regard for the rights and feelings of their peers; less awareness of the need to accept responsibility for their obligations, both as individuals and members of a group; and poor attitudes toward authority, including the failure to understand the needs for rules and regulations in any well-ordered social group and the need for abiding by them. They both resented and rejected authority in the school situation. Their overall social behavior was less acceptable, not simply with teachers, but with peers; they had more difficulty in getting along with peers, both in individual, one-to-one contacts and in group situations, and were less willing or able to treat others courteously and tactfully, and less able to be fair in dealing with them. In return, they were less well-liked and accepted by their peers. They were significantly less likely than their nondelinquent matches to be viewed as dependable, friendly, pleasant, considerate, and fair.

According to Wilson and Herrnstein (1989) "Teachers' ratings of classroom aggressiveness of . . . boys as early as the age of eight predicted later juvenile and adult crime, violent and otherwise. Glueck and Glueck (1950; 1968) in a highly detailed and comprehensive series of analyses of male delinquency found that whether measured in academic, attitudinal, or motivational terms, delinquents perform less adequately than do nondelinquents. The vast majority, i.e., about 90 percent, have established records of misbehavior prior to age 11. Their misbehavior early in school is not only more frequent, but is generally of a more serious nature than that of nondelinquents. Robins and colleagues (1971) found in a study of Afrikan American schoolboys that in all cases adult sociopathy was preceded by some type of antisocial acts or symptoms in childhood, the most common ones being theft, "incorrigible behavior," running away, poor school performance, and truancy.

A study which involved 1,027 children in Sweden presented data which suggests that highly aggressive boys when compared to their less aggressive counterparts, are approximately three times as likely to become criminals in their later lives. The more the boys were evaluated as aggressive by their teachers at ages 10 and 13 (i.e., in terms of fighting, defiance, etc.), the more likely they were to have committed at least one felonious offense by age 26. One in three had multiple convictions for serious offenses.

However, there is good reason to believe that the high correlations between early childhood, elementary school-age aggressiveness and adolescent and young-adult criminality on the part of males can be significantly reduced if these males are given special attention and educational and group-dynamics experiences early enough in their lives. Early childhood educational programs designed to enhance academic and intellectual performances are of special importance in this regard. This is the case not only because a plethora of studies has consistently shown an association between academic competence and criminal behavior, but intelligence (e.g., measured IQ performance) as mediated by the school experience is substantially linked to crime (Hirschi & Handelang, 1977; West & Farrington, 1978; Hirschi, 1966). Of particular interest in this regard is the so-called verbal IQ. Low scores on this measure, contrasted with higher performance IQ scores, have been shown to be significantly associated with social competence, moral development, interpersonal maturity and a tendency to break the law (Wilson & Herrnstein, 1989). In light of these associations it seems apparent that effective academically oriented early childhood education instructional strategies coupled with strategies designed to enhance and maintain personal-social competence skills, good group relations, positive self-esteem, self-acceptance and high levels of positive ethnocultural group identity, would significantly reduce later social maladjustment, maladaptive behavior, delinquency and adult criminality. Academically oriented preschool programs, such as the Perry High School Project, have demonstrably improved these outcomes even when lacking a definite Afrikan-centered curriculum. We think the addition or integration of an academic orientation within an Afrikan-centered curriculum would very significantly improve the Perry High School record.

There are a number of group techniques and behavior modification techniques which are and have been developed for helping aggressive boys. These include "pair therapy," which pairs an extremely aggressive boy with one whose friendship stimulates the more aggressive partner to learn friendship, cooperative relations, negotiation as an alternative to violence (Selwan, In Press). Play groups of grade school children which include an especially aggressive boy may also be used to engage the aggressive member in games which foster cooperation, listening to others, making deals, asking questions, helping and sharing (NYT, 1990).[3] Behavior modification approaches include one that teaches parents to modify or reduce aggressive behavior in their boys through systematic discipline and reward. This approach and similar ones which emphasize operational diagnoses of particular types of aggressive behavior and the prescription of a rather simple series of measurable steps for improving such behavior assume that boys' aggressive and unruly behavior is learned and therefore can be unlearned.

We shall now briefly and broadly outline what Afrikan-centered educational, therapeutic and rehabilitative programs can do to counter the social psychology of oppression as manifested in Black adolescents.

---

3. *The New York Times*, Thursday, February 1, 1990.

Chapter 5

Recommendations

Afrikan-centered Educational Rehabilitation

An Afrikan-centered curriculum includes approaches to countering maladaptive tendencies in school children and adolescents as central to its educational mission. These and related approaches in inextricable conjunction with the Afrikan-centered curriculum's programs for maximizing the intellectual and educational achievement of Afrikan American students; for markedly improving their attendance and reducing their misconduct in school; improving their social and moral/ethical thinking and reasoning; raising their aspirations and expectations, can make the curriculum a major force for minimizing crime and violence and other forms of social malfunctioning in the Afrikan American community and in American society in general.

The larger social, political and systemic problem in American society as a whole, that forms the matrix that gives birth to many of the problems prevalent in inner-city communities, must be addressed at the levels where they occur. This means that Afrikan Americans must continue to press for broad social and cultural changes in American society, changes conducive to the attainment of racial equality, equality of opportunity and achievement, positive interracial relationships and the full remediation of psychological, socioeconomic, sociopolitical and other ills which currently characterize too many Afrikan American communities. The national, state and local governments and their agencies must continue to be pressed to provide fully-adequate family support and child care services, welfare and foster care services, affordable housing; income maintenance assistance; job training and employment training programs; health care and health insurance services; increased yearly childhood and general educational funding; and effective civil and human rights legislation.

On the educational and rehabilitative levels, the focus of Afrikan-centered instructional and psychotherapeutic programs must be the eradication of the "nexus of alienation" in the psyche of Afrikan Americans which reactionarily give rise to the "psychosocial aftereffects" referred to earlier. The operative presence of these psychosocial orientations forms the psychodynamic foundations for the sociopolitical, socioeconomic construction of most of the maladaptive behaviors, including Black-on-Black violence, and the social *dis*eases which impair the mental and material health of the Afrikan American community today. Their presence also must be erased if the Afrikan American and Afrikan communities are to achieve liberation from racial and imperialistic oppression and exploitation. The "nexus of alienation" not only includes alienation itself but also includes the lack of knowledge of the crimogenic nature and operation of American racism and EuroAmerican economic imperialism; the sense of powerlessness; inadequate responses to stereotypical projections; unrealistic and self-destructive desires; internalization of racist attitudes; frustration; displacement; imitation of the aggressor; faulty self-concept; dysfunctional self-esteem; hostility; intellectual, social and personal incompetence; among other stress-producing and misdirective factors.

Broadly speaking, some of the maladaptive psychological predispositions which may motivate Black adolescent males to engage in criminality and violence and some methods for their remediation are noted below.

Maladaptive Psychological Predisposition	Suggested Method for Remediation
Alienation	The reclamation of an Afrikan-centered identity and consciousness; learning how to love the self and others; developing prosocial, cooperative and communalistic skills and orientations.
Crimogenic society	Develop a keen and working knowledge of the ways and means by which American society and EuroAmerican imperialism attempt to inbreed in Afrikan Americans and Pan Afrikans psychological attitudes, behaviors and relations which are self-defeating, self-destructive, and supportive of EuroAmerican oppression; develop the intellectual, personal, social skills necessary to defeat the purposes of the crimogenic society.
Internalization of White racist attitudes towards the self	Construct an efficient perception of reality; develop the analytical ability to critically examine racist distortions of facts, racist myths and to discern malevolent racist intentionalities; develop a deep and working knowledge of the psychology of racism and racist strategies of the EuroAmerican ruling establishment.
Racist projections	Inoculate with deep knowledge of truth and of Afrikan history and culture; knowledge of the psychology of projection, its purpose and function, and of the criminal and immoral origins of American society as well as the evils of imperialism; develop deep self-knowledge and highly positive self-concept and a high level of self-esteem.
Frustration	Develop ability to clearly discern the personal and social sources of frustration; develop problem-solving and task orien-

tation—i.e., approaches to solving causes of frustration and frustration prevention; learn how to use anger and aggressive feelings stemming from frustration positively and constructively; develop creativity, mental and behavioral flexibility and resourcefulness; develop social intelligence, skills and competence; enhance coping strategies for dealing with stress.

Sense of powerlessness

Learn that the powerlessness of Afrikan Americans is an illusion; develop the means of discerning the tremendous power within the grasp of Afrikan people; learn what power is, how it is achieved, developed and controlled; learn the strategies and means by which Afrikan peoples may become truly empowered and influential and by which they must wrest power from the hands of EuroAmerican racists and imperialists, training the youth to develop the personal powers, competencies and skills and to realize the power inherent in ethnic unity and collective action.

Displacement of aggression

Learn the sociopolitical means by which Afrikan Americans are made to perceive each other as primary enemies; learn to confront fears of discerning the real enemies of the Afrikan race and of challenging those enemies; develop which and how economic, political and possibly military means are chosen and utilized to defeat genuine enemies; develop the recognition of the vulnerability of these enemies, that they can be countered, neutralized and defeated; learn how the displacement of anger and aggressive hostility flowing from race-based frustration and reactionary self-hatred and self-alienation onto fellow Afrikans makes matters worse and is ultimately self-destructive.

Egregious self-defeating, self-destructive desires	Learn a new set of Afrikan-centered values; inculcate deep abiding and long-term cultural and personal goals; learn how desires are "manufactured" and produced by the business-commercial-industrial complex and are stimulated and directed by advertising, publicity and public relations; develop the ability to discern when one's desires are being artificially created, manipulated and exploited and the ability to parry these thrusts; learn of the nature of advertising, mass hypnosis, subliminal suggestion, social conditioning, lies, deception and propaganda; learn how the incompetent coping with the effects of racism and frustration may motivate one to seek self-defeating, self-destructive and addictive palliatives instead of real solutions; learn to be productive; develop the personal, social and business skills for attaining significant ownership of the means of production on the part of Afrikan Americans and Pan-Afrikans as a means of satisfying their own needs and desires; develop self-control, self-discipline and the ability to delay gratification; learn the nature and consequences of drug and substance abuse.
Imitation of the racist aggressor	Learn the true nature and intent of role models and reference groups which, on close examination demonstrate that if unwittingly and indiscriminately imitated, will lead to self-defeat and self-destruction; learn of Afrikan heroes and heroines who provide excellent and realistic role models; develop a knowledgeable appreciation of Afrikan high culture, art and cultural models; inculcate a deep, strong, Afrikan-centered consciousness and identity and highly positive Afrikan ethos and ideals.

Negative self-concepts and self-esteem	Develop an adequate knowledge of the achievements and contributions of Afrikan civilizations, cultures and heroes/heroines; develop programs which emphasize Afro-centricity, cooperation and supportive social relations, which utilize techniques for affirmation of self and the development of intellectual, social, personal, and occupational competencies which help to raise self-esteem and self-acceptance.
Tendency toward interpersonal violence	Develop conflict-resolution skills; develop empathetic skills, the ability to take various perspectives on problems and issues; learn alternative means of dealing with problems; inculcate the approaches listed above.

CDC Strategies for Crime Prevention

The U.S. Department of Health and Human Services (1992), specifically the Centers for Disease Control (CDC) which is currently developing guidelines for the prevention of youth violence, has made some preliminary suggestions concerning strategies which may be helpful in preventing or significantly attenuating Black male adolescent violence. These strategies, among a longer list of others, include: adult mentoring, conflict resolution, training in social skills, parenting centers, peer education, public information and education campaigns, preschool programs, therapeutic activities, recreational activities, and work/academic experiences.

Adult Mentoring

Mentors are special role models who provide a positive, caring influence and standard of conduct for young people. Mentors provide models for young people who have no models or they offer alternatives to negative role models. Mentors may reinforce positive attitudes or behaviors children are trying to express. Adult models may be teachers, counselors, friends, and confidants, or simply members of the community. . . . The attention and interest bestowed on the youngsters by people who care, enhance the youth's self-esteem, strengthening the adolescent's ability to choose nonviolent methods to resolve conflicts.

Conflict Resolution Education

Classes in conflict resolution are designed to provide students with the opportunity to develop empathy with others, learn ways to control impulses, develop problem-solving skills, and manage their anger. . . .Courses in conflict resolution have been developed for students in both elementary and high schools.

The methods used to teach conflict resolution usually include role-playing of conflict situation and analyzing the responses and consequences to violence.

Training in Social Skills

Teaching young people social skills provides them with the ability to interact with others in positive and friendly ways . . . .Aspects of social-skills training include self-control, communication skills, forming friendships, resisting peer pressure, being appropriately assertive, and forming good relationships with adults. . . . These educational activities can be conducted in schools, day care settings, after-school programs, and youth organizations.

Parenting Centers

Improving parenting skills through specially designed classes for parents can improve how the parent and child interact. The improvement in this relationship may reduce the risk of child behavior problems and subsequent antisocial behavior. Programs targeted toward parents must address the psychological needs of the parents . . . and the stresses and social supports that can either help or hinder the parent's ability to adapt to the needs of the child.

Peer Education

Programs that use students to teach their peers about violence prevention are a powerful force among adolescents and can be used effectively to shape norms and behavior in this group.

Public Information and Education Campaigns

Public information campaigns reach a broad audience and draw attention to an issue as well as provide a limited amount of information. There is a wide range of media available for these campaigns: public service announcements, educational video programs, appearances on public talk shows, posters, brochures, and other print materials.

Preschool Programs such as Head Start

Project Head Start is designed to help children of low-income families develop a greater degree of social competence through developing the child's intellectual skills, fostering emotional and social development, meeting the child's health and nutritional needs, and involving parents and the community in these efforts.

Therapeutic Activities

There are a number of therapeutic programs available for abused children [and] . . . treatment programs [which] target school-age children with special needs, such as emotional disturbances or as substance abuse problems.

Recreational Activities

Recreational activities offer young people opportunities to spend time in a structured and purposeful environment. . . . [A]ctivities that provide outlets for tension, stress, or anger and opportunities for social interactions and constructive problem-solving are important parts of a program with other violent prevention components.

Work/Academic Experience

Student work and volunteer activities that are supported by community organizations have a positive influence on students. Structured job experiences and volunteer activities connect adolescents with supportive adults who act as role models, mentors, and counselors. . . . Students learn what a community is and how a neighborhood functions while learning the roles they play in society.

The suggested strategies and activities for the prevention of youth violence recommended by the Centers for Disease Control (CDC) are generally and specifically, directly and indirectly, designed to provide children and adolescents with the requisite social, emotional, personal and intellectual skills they need to fulfill their personal potentials and to lead and enjoy productive personal and interpersonal lives. These strategies generally involve modification and reorganization of children's educational and social-interactive experiences in ways which will enable them to prosocially operate in their environments and to achieve their positive life-goals. The CDC has compiled specific programs across the country which utilize specific approaches to adolescent crime prevention. They are listed in the adjoining *Appendix*.

The strategies, therapeutic approaches and methods available for prevention and remediation of youth violence work best when applied prescriptively, i.e., when they are applied to certain homogeneous subgroups of children and adolescents who are predispositionally amenable and especially responsive to a particular strategy, approach or method, or a set or sequence of these treatments (Goldstein, et al., 1980). That is, educational and treatment approaches must be based on a sound and thorough analysis and knowledge of the individual and groups being dealt with and a deep understanding of the range, limitations, strengths and weaknesses of the available approaches and a keen sense of their most likely interactive outcomes.

Remediation of Reactionary Masculinity

We have noted that the adolescent and young adult male's conception of masculinity, of what it means to be a man contribute significantly to their prosocial and/or antisocial behavior. Moreover, we contended that the "reactionary masculinity" of many Afrikan American adolescent males is actualized as delinquent, criminal, often violent behavior. It may also contribute personally and socially unproductive behavior, the exploitative use of others, and to various forms of self-defeating and self-destructive behavior as well. If the characteristics of reactionary masculinity are to be reversed and prevented, then educational, communal and manhood training programs should include as an important part of their programmatic mission the objectives listed below.

- Identify the idea of masculinity with Afrikan-centeredness and consciousness, the idea of Afrikan communalism and a commitment to Afrikan collective goals; a sense of social responsibility and interest.
- Associate masculinity with social service, community uplift and defense; with reason, sensitivity, tolerance, patience, flexibility, creativity, generosity; with productivity, economic self-sufficiency, teamwork, cooperativeness, reliability, trustworthiness, honor and courage; with the ability to attain and maintain feelings of love and intimacy for women, children and other males; with courtliness.
- Encourage males to be motivated by positive drives and to strive for positive goals instead of by negative drives such as inordinate fear, anger, vanity, feelings of inadequacy and inferiority and the need to "prove" masculinity.
- Associate masculinity with self-control, the mastery of knowledge, technique, technology, craft and skills; with intellectual development, self-actualization and positive interpersonal skills.
- Encourage masculine self-definition in terms of productivity and nurturance instead of conspicuous consumption, parasitic exploitation, and faddish fashions.
- Identify masculinity with self-determination, taking responsibility for personal failures as well as successes; with resisting the too-easy temptation to blame others and extenuating circumstances for one's misfortunes or antisocial behavioral tendencies.

- Resist using avoidance, escape, withdrawal and retreat; evasion and denial, projection of false superiority complex, as methods of dealing with problems and painful, unpleasant or unflattering situations.
- Recognize that sexuality, sensuality and pleasurable excitements are important parts of life and among many of its important pursuits but not the whole life, not its only ends; that these passions can be the byproducts of many other productive, positive personal and social vocations and activities; that the mate is the person of equal value to oneself and is due all the deep respect and consideration, freedoms and privileges one demands for oneself; that children are to be nurtured and cared for and not merely utilized to demonstrate sexual prowess and sexual seductiveness.
- Emphasize that family creation, development and maintenance are very serious undertakings and are not to be entered into lightly or blightly.

Training For Liberation and Independence

The central causal factor of maladaptiveness in the Afrikan American community and the Afrikan world community at this time is White American/European domestic and imperialistic domination. Black male adolescent violence and criminality are but aspects or resultants of this larger factor. White American/European domination destroys in Afrikan peoples, especially inner-city Black youth, the sense of mastery over their fate, a key element for attaining and maintaining psychological health, personal and social competence. Dependency bred by domination, the feeling of not being in control or of having a say over what happens in their personal and community lives; feelings of relative powerlessness and the overwhelming desire to achieve a sense of power and control by self-defeating and antisocial means, particularly in the adolescent and young adult male, manifest themselves in ways which adversely affect the physical and mental health, holistic and occupational achievement, social and sexual attitudes and relations of Afrikan American youths and young adults. Black-on-Black violence is one of the critically negative manifestations of an absence of a sense of control bred by oppression.

In essence, our foregoing discussion implies the common-sensical conclusion that feelings of power, competence, mastery, self-control, self-determination and autonomy are of central importance in positive mental health and prosocial behavior. The reasonable assurances that these may be attained with appropriate striving and the presence of media which facilitate their attainment are the necessary factors which conjunctively help to actualize personal and social intellectual, psychological, emotional potential and prevent self-defeating, antisocial behavior. Without such assurance and facilitating factors, the drives toward power, competence, masteries and such are subverted, twisted, expressed counterproductively, and often violently. This is the achievement of the domination of Afrikan males by their European male oppressors and hegemonists. Thus, we must conclude that the most important factor for the remediation and prevention of many problems confronting the Afrikan American and worldwide Afrikan communities is the complete liberation of these communities from White male domination and domination by any other ethnic group. This is one of the central objectives for which Afrikan males must be prepared to accomplish.

Therefore, fundamentals for the education of Afrikan American males must include:

- Early inculcation of Afrikan consciousness and identity; early development of capacities for intense and loyal social relations, networking and collective actions with the ineradicable intention or ending once and for all the control of White men and other ethnic group "pretenders to the throne" of Black oppression.

- Training in reading, math and other academic areas beginning in infancy; in the meditative, spiritual and martial arts; military arts and sciences; history, logic and philosophy; literature, art and culture; science, mathematics, technology; human sociology, psychology and relations.

- Training in how to know their true enemies and in how to express their aggressive feelings outward toward them rather than against themselves.

- Training in self-governance, government and the building of institutions, of nations, and nations-within-nations. They must study *power*, its achievement and preservation as pure subject matter with the view of equaling the power of other men and successfully defending their people against the depredations of others.

- Training and practice in group dynamics, formation and facilitating skills. They must study, understand and practice the special-interest process (e.g., lobbying, political action committees, advisory committees, coalitions), the policy-formation process (e.g., how to formulate and implement policy on larger issues, establish policy planning networks, research and study groups; how to formulate propaganda and shape public opinion and influence the lawmaking process), the candidate-selection and electoral process (e.g., learning to use the electoral rules to influence party politics, establish political parties and caucuses) and the ideology process (e.g., promulgating Afrocentrism, financing and distributing ideological, critical and policy-oriented pamphlets, articles, journals, books, etc.; influencing university and college departments; shaping opinion on foreign policy; education in economics; public interest advertising).

- Training in the very practical techniques of economically gaining control of all Afrikan local and national markets in how to wrest these markets from the hands of other exploitative ethnic groups—by any means necessary.

- Training in how to aggressively move into national and multinational business and economic circles, geopolitical and military alliances so as to be among those who determine the direction of world socioeconomic development and to no longer be the subjects of direction by others.

- Training in the achievement of technological thinking, creativity, organization, and marketing.

- Training in Afrikan values, ethics and morals which by definition are—anti-racist, anti-imperialist, anti-domination, pro-equality, pro-peace and harmony, pro-fraternity, pro-liberty, humanistic, and spiritualistic.

- Training in how to create job and economic opportunities for self and others.

Specific Attitudes and Abilities

- Learn thinking, reasoning, analytical, evaluative and wisdom skills; verbal, oratorical, negotiation and persuasion skills.

- Learn to demonstrate masculinity through the mastery of formal education, technical and professional skills, occupational, romantic, marital and familial success.

- Learn to be respectful of elders, women, children and to be solicitous of others who may be in need of support.

- Learn roles of Afrikan adults and their functions in maintaining the viability and advancing the interests of the Afrikan community.

- Learn parenting and family-husbandry skills; husband-wife, parent-child communications and bonding skills.

Community-based Strategies for Crime Prevention

Overall, criminal violence is a type of *social* encounter or interaction. It reflects various types of social attitudes and relations and therefore always occurs in some explicit or implicit social context. It always has some type of social history or related series of social antecedents. Crime has no useful meaning outside some social or ecological context. Therefore, criminality, its shapes, forms, and functions, its prevalence and incidence, is intimately related to and a social product of the social context or system in which it is manifested. Criminality cannot be understood and explained without understanding how it is induced in significant part by the structure and functionality of the social system which gives it birth and which sustains its life.

When we study criminality across various nations, societies, cultures, subcultures and classes, we note very significant differences in rates, types and other forms of crime which somehow are related to the differences between and within these social systems, strata or categories. An instructive starting point for seeking to discover the causal bases for criminality within a particular society, especially where criminality of a certain general type; e.g., violence, which tends to occur more prevalently in a particular segment of the society than others, is to look at the gross structural and social differences in that society. One may then discover certain consistent and substantial correlations between some of these differences and certain types and levels of criminality.

The United States of America is a society marred by sharp and deep differences, a nation of outstanding inequities between its various social and class groups. Some of its most important group and class inequities exist between White and Black Americans in general; between its upper, middle and working classes (largely White), and its lower, working poor and under classes (largely Black). It is these inequities which are the fertile sources of much of crime in America and its relatively higher violent incidence in the Afrikan American community, particularly in that community's lower socio-economic strata. We can but agree with the noted criminologist Elliot Currie (1985) when he contends:

> It isn't accidental, then, that among developed countries, the United States is afflicted simultaneously with the worst rates of violent crime, the widest spread of income inequality, and the most severe public policies toward the disadvantaged. The industrial societies that have escaped our extremes of criminal violence tend either to have highly-developed public sectors with fairly generous systems of income support, relatively well developed employment policies and other cushions against "the forces of the market. . . ."

Currie goes on to compile evidence which demonstrates clearly "that higher homicide rates [are] linked with several measures of economic inequity and other disparities in income, nutritional consumption, education, and the like." Concentrated poverty, the single greatest risk factor, interactively combined with racism, the absence of good health services, dysfunctional schools, irrational and discriminatory employment and income policies, unresponsive and inadequate social services, provides a potent mixture of malefactors which often explodes with violent and destructive repercussions. Obviously, these factors must be markedly improved and the American social system radically reformed if the problems of Black-on-Black adolescent violence and criminality along with the other social ailments of Black America are to be cured and prevented. Therefore, the Afrikan American community must organize itself, strengthen its resolve and unflinchingly utilize all of its considerably influential economic social and political power to transform the American social system for its own communal and America's own national betterment. The Afrikan American community has demonstrated its ability to change the American landscape on a number of important occasions, most notably during the antebellum and civil war era and the 1960s. It can do so again if it chooses to do so.

The Black American
Political Economy and Crime

While individual, one-on-one, and group educational, preventive, remedial, rehabilitative and psychotherapeutic approaches can be effective, if effectively and appropriately applied, they do not deal directly with the large sociopolitical and socioeconomic variables which are the root causes of the largest portion of group and individual problems. Unless basic social problems engendered by a dysfunctional socioeconomic system are resolved, the strategies and activities alluded to above can only be ameliorative or provide symptomatic relief at best. They could never turn back the flood of children and adolescents with special problems so massively produced by a malfunctional social system as is current in the United States today. Therefore, broad national and community-institutional reforms are necessary (in combination with specific approaches and programs) for the meaningful prevention of Black adolescent violence and crime. Recommendations by Currie (1985) for helping to prevent crime in America may serve as an example to the type of national and community measures which may be undertaken to begin to very significantly reduce criminal violence in America and especially in the Afrikan-American community. The recommendations by Currie include the following:

- Exploration and development of intensive rehabilitation programs for youthful offenders, preferably in local community or in a supportive institutional milieu.
- Community-based, comprehensive family support programs, emphasizing local participation and respect for cultural diversity.
- Improved family planning services and support for teenaged parents.
- Paid work leaves and more accessible child care for parents with young children, to ease the conflicts between child-rearing and work.

- High-quality, early-prevention programs for disadvantaged children.
- Expanded community dispute-resolution programs.
- Comprehensive, locally based services for victims of domestic violence.
- Intensive job training, perhaps modeled along the lines of supported work, designed to prepare the young and the displaced for stable careers.
- Strong support for equity in pay and conditions, aimed at upgrading the quality of low-paying jobs.
- Substantial *permanent* public and public-private job creation in local communities, at wages sufficient to support a family breadwinner, especially in areas of clear and pressing social needs like public safety, rehabilitation, child care and family support.
- Universal — and generous — income support for families headed by individuals outside the paid labor force.

In addition to Currie's recommendations, major strides in eliminating or greatly reducing Black adolescent violence and crime can be made if national governmental efforts were successfully undertaken to markedly improve the social context in which many Black inner-city adolescents live today. The positive transformation of this crimogenic context, in conjunction with Afrikan-centered education and consciousness, should go far toward making the Afrikan American community violence and crime free.

We must also note that violence and criminality within the Afrikan American community not only reflect socioeconomic distortions and inequalities within the larger White-dominated American social system but economic and therefore social dislocations in the Black-dominated social subsystem itself. In addition to relatively lower rates of participation in the general labor market due to historical and contemporary racism and "human capital deficits [i.e., educated, trained, skilled workers] that continued to limit qualifications of black workers . . . " (Swinton, 1990), the Afrikan American community is further

impeded by its severely limited wealth and business ownership and a self-defeating consumer orientation. That is, the
local ownership of portions of businesses and public corporations in the larger economy are essentially negligible given the
size and the learning/spending power of this community. The
Afrikan American community is virtually totally dis-invested
and shamelessly economically exploited by other ethnic
groups who own and control its local markets and real estate
and thereby remove billions of dollars daily from its coffers,
robbing it of its wealth and the concomitant power which
accompanies it. The relative failure of the Afrikan American
community to invest in the wealth-producing instruments
offered by the general American market economy means a
devastating loss of opportunities to increase its socioeconomic
well-being and its politico-economic power. Moreover, the
alarming and overwhelming tendency of Afrikan Americans
to spend huge amounts of money and consume indiscriminately with and from non-black businesses and service establishments who contribute little or nothing to their economic
growth and stability, almost completely destroys that community's ability to "do for self" and use its own rather consider-
able potential to solve many of its problems such as Black-on-
Black adolescent violence and criminality.

As observed by Swinton (1990), "These disadvantages in
ownership and we may add, [spending/consumption pat-
terns] generate the disadvantages observed in self-employ-
ment, property, and retirement income." Through its indis-
criminate spending and consumer habits the Afrikan American community enriches and subsidizes the families and
children of other ethnic groups, thereby helping to economically stabilize their communities, reduce their rates of violence
and crime, and enhancing their accumulation of wealth and
political power while dis-investing and empowering its own
families and children economically, devitalizing itself, increasing its rates of violence and crime, and creating deficits in its
economic and political power.

The Afrikan American community could very markedly reduce crime, violence, miseducation, poverty, etc., if it would become conscious of itself as a nation-within-a-nation, of its spending, consumption and investment patterns and organize its consciousness in ways which best serve its own material and nonmaterial interests. It must remove predatory merchants and service establishments from its internal markets and assume ownership and control of those markets; it must monitor how and how much it spends with large, national and multinational companies and the contributions these companies make to the community, its institutions and economic well-being and spend or not spend with them accordingly; it must organize itself as national and international economic network and invest its wealth in its local markets, the national markets and the international markets, especially in countries, nations and areas where Afrikan people predominate. The process of accomplishing these ends will radically and positively transform the Afrikan American/Pan Afrikan socio-economic landscape and in its wake, transform its violent and delinquent youths into productive, prosocial community members and adults.

The approaches discussed above and related approaches, as well as new and innovative approaches derived from clear observation of the behavior of Afrikan American boys based on a thorough understanding Afrikan/Afrikan American history, culture, sociology, can be of very significant importance in reversing the violent trends now prevalent in the Afrikan American and Pan-Afrikan communities, and to prepare them to do their part in achieving the liberation of Afrikan peoples and to contribute to the liberation of Humankind as a whole. ∎

Appendix

Organizational Strategies and Activities
for Preventing Black Adolescent Violence[4]

Educational Strategies: Mentoring

NAME	TARGET GROUP
Black Male Youth Project 1510 9th St., N.W. Washington DC 20001 (202) 332-0213	Males, ages 11-17
Project 2000 Morgan State University School of Education in Urban Studies 322 Jenkins Hall Baltimore, MD 21239 (301) 444-3275	Elementary school-age males, from single-par- ent, female-headed homes
Project Image 765 E. 69th St., Chicago, IL 60637 (312) 324-8700	African American males ages 8-18
Project PEACE 534 E. 69th St. 1st fl. Chicago, IL 60653 (312) 791-4768	Elementary and high school students near public housing
Project PEACE 605 N. Eutaw Street Baltimore, MD 21201 (301) 685-8316	High-risk youth in fifth, sixth, and seventh grades
Young Men's Project 3030 W. Harrison St. Chicago, Il 60612 (312) 265-7440 6000 S. Wentworth Avenue Chicago, Il 60621 (312) 225-4433	African American males

4. Adaptation of a list compiled by the Centers for Disease Control (CDC) 1992 (Draft).

NAME	TARGET GROUP
Black Male Youth Project 1510 9th Street, N.W. Washington DC 20001 (202) 332-0213	Males, ages 11-17
Project 2000 Morgan State University of Education in Urban Studies 322 Jenkins Hall Baltimore, MD 21239 (301) 444-3275	Elementary school-age males, from single-parent, female-headed homes
Youth at Risk 3059 Fillmore St., San Francisco, CA 94123 (415) 673-0717	Youth, ages 15-20

Educational Strategies: Conflict Resolution

NAME	TARGET GROUP
Boston Conflict Resolution Program Box 271, 523 N. Broadway Nyack, NY 10960 (914) 358-4601	Early elementary school children and teachers
Children's Creative Response to Conflict	Early elementary school children
Grant Middle School Conflict Resolution Training 2400 Grant Boulevard Syracuse, NY 13208 (315) 435-4433	Students
Hawaii Meditation Program Univ. of Hawaii at Manoa, West Hall Annex 2, Room 222 1776 University Ave. Honolulu, HI 96822	Students
House of Umoja Boystown 1410 N. Frazier Street Philadelphia, PA 19131 (215) 473-5893	Potential gang members

NAME	TARGET GROUP
Resolving Conflict Creativity Program 163 Third Ave., #239 NY, NY 10003 (212) 260-6290	Children and youth in grades K-12
Santa Fe Mountain Center State of New Mexico	High risk youth First offenders
School Initiatives Program 149 Ninth Street, San Francisco, CA 94103 (415) 552-1250	Students
Urban Interpersonal Violence Injury Control Project Kansas City, Missouri	High-risk youth, usually referred through courts or social services
Violence Prevention Project 1010 Massachusetts Ave. Boston, MA 02118 (617) 534-5196	Adolescents
Voyageur Outward Bound School 500 W. Madison Street, Suite 2100 Chicago, IL 60606 (312) 715-0550	Gang members, 13-17 years of age

Educational Strategies: Training in Life and Social Skills

NAME	TARGET GROUP
Barron Assessment and Counseling Center 25 Walk Hill Street, Jamaica Plan MA 02130 (617) 469-4606	Weapon carriers
Boston Conflict Resolution Program Box 271, 523 N. Broadway Nyack, NY 10960 (914) 358-4601	Elementary school children and teachers

NAME	TARGET GROUP
Channeling Children's Anger 4545 42nd St. N.W. Suite 311 Washington, DC 20016 (202) 364-7111	Junior and senior students. Professionals who work with young people and their families
Chicanos por la Causa 1112 E. Buckeye Road Phoenix, AZ 85034 (602) 257-0700	High risk youth
Children's Creative Response to Conflict [no address]	Early elementary school children
Community Youth Gang Services Project 144 S. Fetterly Ave. Los Angeles, CA 90022 (213) 632-2947	Gang members Potential gang members
Early Adolescent Helper Program 25 West 43rd Street, Rm. 620 NYC NY 10036 (212) 642-2947	Adolescents, ages 10-15
Gang Peace 32 Gaston Street, Roxbury, MA (714) 535-3722	Gang members Potential gang members
Gang Prevention and Intervention Program 1602 S. Brookhurst St. Anaheim, CA 92804 (714) 535-3722	School-age youth
Good Grief Program 295 Longwood Ave. Boston, MA 02115 (617) 232-8390	Children who experience a death of a family member or friend through violence
House of Umoja Boystown 1410 N. Frazier Philadelphia, PA 19131 (215) 473-5893	Potential gang members

NAME	TARGET GROUP
HAWK Federation Manhood Development and Training Program 155 Filbert Street, #202 Oakland, California 94607 (415) 836-3245	Adolescent African Americans
Milwaukee Public Schools P.O. Drawer, 10K, Milwaukee, WI 53201 (414) 475-8393	African American males
"OUCH" Theatre 500 N. Robert Street, Suite 220 St. Paul, MN 55101 (612) 227-9660	Elementary school children
The Paramount Plan 16400 Colorado Ave., Paramount, CA 90723 (213) 220-2140	Potential gang members
PATHS: Providing Alternative Thinking Strategies University of Washington Seattle, WA 98195	Early elementary school children
Philadelphia Injury Prevention Program 500 S. Broad Street Philadelphia, PA 19146 (215) 875-5661	Gang members
Project SPIRIT 600 New Hampshire Ave. N.W., Ste. 650 Washington, DC 20037 (202) 333-3060	Children and parents
Santa Fe Mountain Center State of New Mexico	High-risk youth First offenders
Southeast Community Day Center School 9525 E. Imperial Highway Downey, CA 90242 (213) 922-6821	Juvenile offenders

NAME	TARGET GROUP
Southeastern Michigan Spinal Cord Injury System 261 Mack Avenue, Detroit, MI 48201 (313) 745-9740	High school students
Teens, Crime, and the Community National Crime Prevention Council 733 15th Street, N.W., Suite 540 Washington DC 20005 (205) 393-7141	Students
Urban Interpersonal Violence Injury Control Project Kansas City, Missouri	High-risk youth, usually referred through courts and services
Viewpoints Training Program Center for Research on Aggression, Dept. of Psychology P.O. Box 4348 M/C 285, Chicago, IL 60680 (312) 413-2624	Violent youth
Voyageur Outward Bound School 500 W. Madison Street, Suite 2100 Chicago, IL 60606 (312) 715-0550	Gang members, 13-17 years of age
Where Have All the Children Gone? 2051 W. Grand Boulevard Detroit, MI 48208 (313) 895-4000	Students, 10-17 years of age
The Yale-New Haven Social Competence Promotion Program New Haven, Connecticut	Students
Young Men's Project 3030 W. Harrison St. Chicago, IL 60612 (312) 265-7440 60000 S. Wentworth Ave., Chicago, Il 60621 (312) 225-4433	African American males

NAME	TARGET GROUP
Youth at Risk 3059 Fillmore Street San Francisco, CA 94123 (415) 673-0717	Youth, ages 15-20
Youth Development, Inc. 1710 Centro Familiar, S.W. Albuquerque, NM 87105 (505) 831-6038	All ages (from 3-year-olds to youth in early 20s)
102nd Street Elementary School Los Angeles, California	Children who experience a death in the family member or friend through violence

Educational Strategies: Firearm Safety

NAME	TARGET GROUP
Kids + Guns = A Deadly Equation 1450 Northeast 2nd Ave., Rm. 904 Miami, FL 33132 (305) 995-1986	Students
Public Information Campaign Charlotte, N.C. police department	Public

Educational Strategies: Recreational Activities

NAME	TARGET GROUP
Challengers Boys Group 5029 S. Vermont Avenue Los Angeles, CA 90037 (213) 971-6141	Males and females ages 6-17
Chicago Commons Association 915 N. Walcott, Chicago, IL 60622 (312) 342-5330	Gang members Potential gang members

NAME	TARGET GROUP
Community Youth Services 144 S. Fetterly Ave. Los Angeles, CA	Gang members Potential gang members
House of Umoja Boystown 1410 N. Frazier St. Philadelphia, PA 19131	Potential gang members
Santa Fe Mountain Center State of New Mexico	High-risk youth First offenders
Urban Interpersonal Violence Injury Control Project Kansas City, Missouri	High-risk youth, usually referred through courts or social services
Youth Development, Inc. 1710 Centro Familiar, S.W. Albuquerque, NM 87105 (505) 831-6038	All ages (from 3-year-olds to youth in early 20s)

Environmental Strategies: Work Opportunities

NAME	TARGET GROUP
Chicago Commons Association 917 N. Walcott Chicago, IL 60622 (312) 342-5330	Gang members Potential gang members
Chicano por la Causa	Juvenile offenders
Community Youth Gang Services 144 S. Fetterly Ave. Los Angeles, CA 90022 (213) 266-4264	Gang members Potential gang members
Early Adolescent Program Helper 25 West 43rd Street, Room 620 NY, NY 10036 (212) 643-2947	Adolescents, ages 10-15

NAME	TARGET GROUP
Gang Peace 32 Gaston Street Roxbury, MA (416) 443-7391	Gang members Potential gang members
Southeast Community Day Center School 9525 East Imperial Highway Downey, CA 90242	Juvenile offenders
Youth Development, Inc. 1710 Centro Familiar, S.W. Albuquerque, NM 87105	All ages (from 3-year-olds to youth in early 20s)

Environmental Strategies: Therapeutic Activities

NAME	TARGET GROUP
House of Umoja Boystown 1410 N. Frazier St. Philadelphia, PA 19131 215 473-5893	Potential gang members
Philadelphia Injury Prevention Program 500 S. Broad Street Philadelphia, PA 19146 (215) 875-5661	Gang members
Save Our Sons and Daughters 453 Martin Luther Boulevard Detroit, MI 48201 (303) 833-3030	Parents Public
Violence Prevention Project 1010 Massachusetts Ave. Boston, MA 02118 (617) 534-5196	Adolescent

Bibliography

Bell, C., & E. Jenkins, 1990. "Preventing Black Homicide" in *The State of Black America 1990*. New York: National Urban League, pp.143-155.

Centers for Disease Control (CDC), U.S. Department of Health and Human Resources 1991. *Guidelines for Prevention of Youth Violence: A Community Approach* (Draft Copy), Atlanta.

Conger, J., and W. Miller, 1966. *Personality, Social Class, and Delinquency*. New York: Wiley.

Cruse, H. 1987. *Plural But Equal: A Critical Study of Blacks and Minorities and American's Plural Society*. New York: William Morrow/Quill.

Currie, E. 1985. *Confronting Crime: An American Challenge*. New York: Pantheon Books.

Dietz, P.1987. "Patterns in Human Violence" in R.E. Hales & A.J. France (eds.), *Psychiatric Update: The American Psychiatric Association Annual Review, Vol. 5*. Washington, D.C.: American Psychiatric Press.

Federal Bureau of Investigation. 1987. *Crime in the United States: 1986*. Washington, D.C.: U.S. Department of Justice.

Fenichel, O. 1945. *The Psychoanalytical Theory of Neuroses*. New York: W.W. Norton.

Garrow, D. 1981. *The FBI and Martin Luther King, Jr.* New York: Penguin Books.

Gilmore, D. 1990. *Manhood in the Making: Cultural Concepts of Masculinity*. New Haven: Yale University Press.

Glueck, S., and E. Glueck, 1968. *Delinquents and Nondelinquents in Perspective*. Cambridge, MA: Harvard University Press.

_____, 1950. *Unraveling Juvenile Delinquency*. Cambridge, MA: Harvard University Press.

Goldstein, A., R. Sprafkin, N. Gershaw, & Klein, 1980. *Skillstreaming the Adolescent: A Structured Learning Approach to Teaching Prosocial Skills*. Champaign, Illinois: Research Press.

Gough, H. 1948. "A Sociological Theory of Psychopathy" in *American Journal of Sociology, 53*: 356-366.

Hilliard A., L. Payton-Stewart, & L. Williams (eds.) 1990. *Infusion of African and African American Content in the School Curriculum*. Proceeding of the First Nation Conference, October 1989. Morristown, New Jersey: Aaron Press.

Hirschi, T. & M. Hindelang, 1977. "Intelligence and Delinquency: A Revisionist View" in *American Sociological Review, 42,* 571-587.

Hirschi, T. 1969. *Causes of Delinquency.* Berkeley, CA: University of California Press.

Lowen, A. 1958. *The Language of the Body.* New York: Collier-Macmillan.

McCord, W. & J. McCord, 1964. *The Psychopath: An Essay on the Criminal Mind.* Princeton, New Jersey: Van Nostrand.

Millon, T. 1969. *Modern Psychopathology: A Biosocial Approach to Maladaptive Learning and Functioning.* Philadelphia: W.B. Saunders.

Reich, W. 1945. *Character Analysis.* 3rd ed. New York: Farrar, Straus & Giroux.

"Report of the Commissioner's Task Force on Minorities: Equity and Excellence." July 1989. *A Curriculum of Inclusion.*

Riordan, C. 1990. *Girls and Boys in School: Together or Separate?* New York: Teachers College Press.

Robins, R., G. Murphy, R. Woodruff, Jr. & L. King, 1971. "The Adult Psychiatric Status of Black Schoolboys" in *Archives of General Psychiatry, 24:* 338-345.

Rosenberg, M. & J. Mercy, 1986. "Homicide: Epidemiologic Analysis at the National Level" in *Bulletin of the New York Academy of Medicine, 62:* 376-399.

"Secretary's Task Force on Black and Minority Health" in *Report of the Secretary's Task Force on Black and Minority Health, Volume 1, Executive Summary.* 1985. Washington, DC: U.S. Dept. of Health and Human Services.

Selwan, R. In Press. *Making A Friend.* Chicago: Univ. of Chicago Press.

Sills, D., ed. 1968. "Assimilation" in *International Encyclopedia of the Social Sciences.* Vol. 1. New York: Macmillan/Free Press.

Swinton, D. 1989. "Economic Status of Black Americans During the 1980s: A Decade of Limited Progress" in *The State of Black America 1990.* New York: National Urban League, Inc. pp. 25-52.

Wallace, A. 1970. *Culture and Personality.* 2nd ed. NY.: Random House.

West, D. and D. Farrington, 1973. *Who Becomes Delinquent?* London: Heinemann Education Books.

Willi, J. 1982. *Couples in Collusion: The Unconsciousness Dimension in Partner Relationships.* Claremont, CA: Hunter House.

Wilson, Amos. 1990. *Black-on-Black Violence: The Psychodynamics of Black Self-Annihilation in Service of White Domination.* New York: Afrikan World InfoSystems.

Wilson, J. and R. Herrnstein, 1985. *Crime and Human Nature.* New York: Simon & Schuster/Touchstone.

Recommended Reading

Alexander, Michelle, *The New Jim Crow: Mass Incarceration in the Age of Colorblindness*. New York: The New Press, 2010.

Baptist, Edward, *The Half Has Never Been Told: Slavery and the Making of American Capitalism:* New York: Basic Books, 2014.

Black, Edwin, *War Against the Weak: Eugenics and America's Campaign to Create a Master Race*. Washington DC: Dialog Press, 2012.

Blackmon, Douglas, A., *Slavery by Another Name: The Re-Enslavement of Black Americans from the Civil War to World War II*. New York: Anchor Books, 2008.

Coates, Ta-Nehisi, *Between the World and Me*. New York: Spiegel and Grau, 2015.

Ewing, Adam, *The Age of Garvey: How a Jamaican Activist Created a Mass Movement & Changed Global Black Politics*. New Jersey: Princeton University Press, 2014.

Hilliard, Asa G., *The Maroon Within Us: Selected Essays on American Community Socialization*. Baltimore: Black Classic Press, 1995.

Isenberg, Nancy, *White Trash: The 400-Year History of Class in America*. New York:Viking, 2016.

Israel, Elisha J., *Killing Black Innocents: The Program to Control "African American" Reproduction* (from slavery's end to the present-day self-inflicted genocide) CreateSpace Internet Platform, 2012.

Jacoby, Susan, *Strange Gods: A Secular History of Conversion*. New York: Pantheon Books, 2016.

Johnson, David Cay, ed., *Divided: The Perils of Our Growing Inequality*. New York: The New Press, 2014.

Loewen, James W., *Sundown Towns: A Hidden Dimension of American Racism*. New York: Touchtone Books, 2006.

_____ , *Lies My Teacher Told Me: Everything Your American History Textbooks Got Wrong*. New York: Touchtone Books, 2007.

Maxwell, William J., *F.B. Eyes: How J. Edgar Hoover's Ghostreaders Framed Afrikan American Literature*. New Jersey: Princeton Univ. Press, 2015.

Roberts, Dorothy, *Killing the Black Body: Race, Reproduction and the Meaning of Liberty*. New York: Random House, 1998.

Stone, Oliver and Peter Koznick, *The Untold History of the United States*. New York: Gallery Books, 2012.

Sublette, Ned and Constance, *The American Slave Coast: A History of the Slave-Breeding Industry*. Chicago: Lawrence Gill, 2016.

Washington, Harriet, *Medical Apartheid: The Dark History of Medical Experimentation on Black Americans from Colonial Times to the Present*. New York: Anchor Books, 2006.

Index

Adler, 107, 109
adult mentoring, 132
Afrikans, not as Christians, 30
aftereffects, racism's psychosocial, 84, 94, 128
aggression, 85, 108, 110, 130, 152
anal-receptive, 109
alienation, 45, 86, 90, 97, 103, 107, 128, 129, 131
ambivalence, 85
American dilemma, 16
Amsterdam News, 12, 18
anger, 19, 44, 50, 85, 100, 115, 130, 133, 134, 136, 150
anxiety, 86, 87, 96
apathy, 84-86, 111
arrest statistics, 13
assimilationism, 10
Atkinson, 91

Baltimore schools, 123
behavior, 5, 9, 22, 25, 26, 42, 43, 49, 58, 64, 81, 82, 84, 86, 91, 109, 113, 116, 130; antisocial, 75-77, 104, 117, 120, 123, 133, 135-138 cognitive, 90, 119; criminal, 1, 2; maladaptive, 126-128; sociopathoid, 95, 98, 100-103; white hypocritical, 98
Bell, 83
big man, 36
Black music, as World music, 58
boys
academic achievement, 123; aggressive, 124-25; arrests, 14-16; into giver of sustenance, 44; in same-sex schools, 123; school suspensions, 12; training, 29, 32, 36, 49, 53, 112, 114, 116

cancer, as political syndrome, 7
cattle, 30, 32, 34, 36
Centers for Disease Control (CDC), 82, 83, 132, 135, 147
character assassination, 82
childhood, 102, 108, 125, 128
Christianity, 30, 31
chronic suspiciousness, 46
circumcision, 32
college student enrollees, 15
compensatory striving, 87
conflict resolution, 132, 133, 148, 149
Conger, 124
consciousness, 5, 41, 65, 76, 77, 90, 94, 103, 106, 110, 129, 132, 136, 138, 144, 146
constant job of becoming, 62
consumer, 88, 107, 109, 145
mentality, 53; to producer, 35, 36, 53
consumption, 54, 61, 88, 142, 145, 146
conspicuous, 53, 136
Correctional Association of New York, 12
courage, 45, 107, 108, 112, 115, 136
cowardice, criminal, 34, 40, 109
crack (cocaine), 1, 6, 28, 40, 75
crime, 2, 13, 14, 56, 57, 75, 80, 81, 94, 100, 108, 116, 124, 125, 127, 132, 135, 141-146, 152, 165, 166
criminality, 1, 2, 10, 13, 28, 56, 75-77, 80, 81, 84, 111, 117, 125, 126, 128, 137, 141, 142, 144, 145
as coward's heroism, 109
crimogenic, 80, 82, 128, 129, 144
curriculum, 79, 118, 121, 126, 127
Currie, 142-144

Daily News, 123
death-wish, 7

**Study Materials and
Book Promotion Ads**

Books by Afrikan World InfoSystems

Black-on-Black Violence:
The Psychodynamics of Black Self-Annihilation in Service of White Domination

A piercing insight into the nature and causes of Black-on-Black violence.

ISBN 978-1-879164-00-0
PB. Pages: 232
$19.00

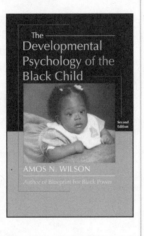

The Developmental Psychology of the Black Child
Second Edition

The best selling text on Black child development.

ISBN 978-1-879164-13-2
PB. Pages: 320
$20.00

Afrikan-Centered Consciousness Versus The New World Order: Garveyism in the Age of Globalism
(illustrated with maps)

A splendid introductory text on the survival of Afrikan Nationalism in the face of the new imperialism.

ISBN 978-1-879164-09-4
PB. Pages: 160
$15.00

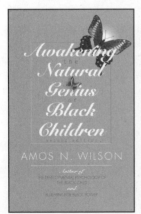

Awakening the Natural Genius of Black Children
Third Edition

In this insightful text Dr. Wilson asserts, "Black children have a natural head start," and sets out to prove it.

ISBN 978-1-879164-01-7
PB. Pages: 160
$15.00

Books by Afrikan World InfoSystems

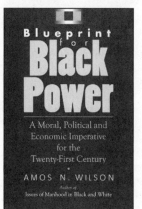

Blueprint For Black Power: A Moral, Political, and Economic Imperative for the Twenty-First Century

Masterful, nothing less than brilliant!

ISBN 978-1-879164-06-2
PB. pages: 912
$46.00

ISBN 978-1-879164-07-9
HC. Pages: 912
$75.00

Issues of Manhood in Black and White: An Imcisive Look into Masculinity and the Societal Definition of Afrikan Man

A ground-breaking text, a leader in its field!

ISBN 978-1-879164-14-7
PB. Pages: 184
$16.00

Distorted Truths: The Bastardization of Afrikan Cosmology
S. K. Damani Agyekum

A forceful and intelligent approach exposing Western bastardization of Afrikan Cosmology throughout history.

ISBN 978-879164-12-3
PB. Pages: 512
$32.00

The Falsification of Afrikan Consciousness: Eurocentric History, Psychiatry and the Politics of White Supremacy

A multi part series that boldly challenges entrenched Eurocentric institutions.

ISBN 978-1-879164-02-7
PB. Pages: 160
$15.00

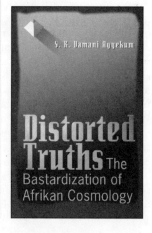

Profiles of Other Acclaimed Books by AWIS

Blueprint For Black Power: *A Moral, Economic and Political Imperative for the 21ˢᵗ Century* details a master plan for the power revolution necessary for Black survival in the 21ˢᵗ century. It illuminates that though Afrikan Americans take home nearly $500 billion yearly of the trillions they generate, they retain a mere 5% of this income. Viewed as a nation their economy would be 8ᵗʰ or 9ᵗʰ largest in the world! Wilson argues that were it to view itself a *de facto* nation and organize as such then its incessant scourge of poverty, disemployment, crime, mis-education, misleadership, consumerism and powerlessness would be drastically reduced. He deconstructs and delegitimates the U.S. governmental, corporate and power-elite structures, debunks ethnocentrism, global imperial capitalism and their portent for Afrikan communities locally and peoples globally. Furthermore, he roundly castigates the ineptitude of Black sycophantic religious/political leadership.

Blueprint warns of Black obsolescence in the coming millennia! It mandates and instructs searing, radical approaches and opportunities for true global Black Power. ✦Available in Library HB /PB. PAGES: 912

Afrikan-centered Consciousness versus the New World Order: *Garveyism in the Age of Globalism* consists of two spellbinding lectures buttressed by a scintillating overview. This modest text challenges the all too pervasive assumption and false perception that the "New World Order" is somehow ordained; that if Afrikan people are to progress, they have no other alternative but to remain colonized by white Western interests. This of course is patently false. Dr. Wilson debunks this myth with an insightful analysis of the Legacy of Marcus Garvey and the proven validity of Afrikan-centered consciousness as necessary psychological and material tools in the struggle for true liberation.

Wilson puts forth his argument in ways that grab the general reader and simultaneously reduces the much-touted strategic thinking of the proponents of the New World Order to the mere newspeak it really is. This text has become the perfect complement to the understanding of *Blueprint For Black Power*. PB. PAGES: 160

Awakening the Natural Genius of Black Children. Afrikan children are naturally precocious and gifted. They begin life with a "natural head start." Intelligence is not fixed at birth. There is clear evidence that the quality of children's educational experiences during infancy and early childhood are substantially related to their measured intelligence, academic achievement and social behavior. Wilson reveals the daily routines, child-rearing practices, parent-child interactions, games and play materials, parent training and pre-school programs which have made demonstrably outstanding and lasting differences in the intellectual, academic and social performance of Afrikan American children. Updated with a new foreword this text remains a *tour de force*.
PB. PAGES: 160

Black-on-Black Violence*: The Psychodynamics of Black Self-Annihilation in Service of White Domination* represents a distinct milestone in criminology and Afrikana Studies. Its main thesis is that the operational existence of *Black-on-Black* violence in the United States is psychologically and economically mandated by the White American-dominated status quo. The criminalization of the Black American male is a psychopolitically engineered process geared to maintain dependency and relative powerlessness of the Afrikan American and Pan-Afrikan communities. Wilson, beyond blaming the victimizer exposes the psychosocial and intrapsychical dynamics of *Black-on-Black* criminality. PB. Pages: 232

The Developmental Psychology of the Black Child, 2ND EDITION

- Are Black and White children the same?
- Is the Black child a White child who happens to be "painted" Black?
- Are there any significant differences in the mental and physical development of Black and White children?
- Do Black parents socialize their children to be inferior to White children?

This pioneering book looks at these and other related controversial questions from an Afrikan perspective. The topics of growth, development and education are scholarly explored.

Recently expanded, updated and indexed, this text was fortified with new foreword and user-friendly typography.

PB. PAGES: 320

The Falsification of Afrikan Consciousness: Eurocentric History, Psychiatry and the Politics of White Supremacy

is a triple feature. Part I, *Eurocentric Historiography in the European Oppression of Afrikan People* was among the first contemporary analyses delineating the role that Eurocentric history-writing plays in rationalizing European oppression of Afrikan peoples and in falsifying Afrikan consciousness. It explicates why we should study history; how history-writing shapes the psychology of peoples and individuals; how this history as mythology creates, in Afrikans, historical amnesia that robs their material, mental, social and spiritual wherewithal for overcoming poverty and oppression.

Part II, *Eurocentric Political Dogmatism*, contends that the alleged mental and behavioral maladaptiveness of oppressed Afrikan peoples is a political-economic necessity for the maintenance of White domination and imperialism. It indicts the Eurocentric mental health establishment for entering into collusion with the Eurocentric political establishment to egregiously oppress and exploit Afrikan peoples by mis-diagnosing, mislabeling and mistreating reactions to oppression.

PB. Pages: 160

A NEW RELEASE

Distorted Truths: *The Bastardization of Afrikan Cosmology* deconstrcts Western thought and Judaeo-Christian practice by exposing their theft, outright bastardization and usurpation of Afrikan cosmology and history. It reframes Diop's *Civilization or Barbarism* and George James' *Stolen Legacy* while painstakingly unveiling Western scholars fraudulent search for white supremacy, their obfuscation of Afrika's origin and contribution to world culture and civilization.

It retraces the development of civilization across time and cultures through extensive use of Grimaldi out-migrations from Afrika into Europe and beyond. He profiles the Dogon, Bambara, Mbuti, Twa, San, and Khoi as existing cosmological systems, cementing how Afrikan thought, ancestral honor, and body-soul development interweave with land use, human becoming (initiation), animal and earth custodianship to create a balanced and abiding relationship between the human being and Nature.

Aptly illustrated, this text courses us through astronomy, archeology, paleontology, anthropology and related disciplines; pre- and post-dynastic Nile Valley and other Afrikan cultures; Asiatic invasions and Greco-Roman-Byzantine domination — which incidentally gave birth and evolvement to our *modern* Christ concept. Agyekum summarizes the impact of Christendom's rise as punctuated by the closing of Nile Valley educational schools (or Egyptian Mystery System) by Roman rulers, which sowed the seeds for Western Asian and European conquests, expansionism, bastardized worldviews, derisive cosmology and colonialism.

Distorted Truths adds to a growing canon crafted to reclaim Afrikan worldview, promote dignity, clarity, unity and lasting Afrikan power.   PB. PAGES: 512

✦ A *comprehensive* read!!! See our AWIS ORDER FORM for details.

Dr. Amos N. Wilson 1941-1995

About the Author

Professor Amos N. Wilson is a former social caseworker, supervising probation officer, psychological counselor, training administrator in the New York City Department of Juvenile Justice, and Assistant Professor of Psychology at the City University of New York.

Born in Hattiesburg, Mississippi, in 1941, Amos Nelson Wilson completed his undergraduate degree in psychology at Morehouse College in Atlanta, Georgia. He migrated to New York where he mastered at Fordham University *and* The New School For Social Research before attaining his doctorate from Fordham, Bronx, New York, in the field of General Theoretical Psychology.

Dr. Wilson taught courses in general, developmental, adolescent, abnormal, social, personality and cognitive psychology; thinking and writing skills development; provided personal and academic counsel; researched and designed youth and adult rehabilitation programs, etcetera. His ambitions and magnanimity furthered as he availed himself for numerous appearances at educational, cultural and political organizations and universities throughout the U.S., also Canada and the Caribbean. He readily tutored at the Harlem School of Africana Studies, a communiversity founded by the eminent First World Alliance. Brother Amos' activities transcended academia into the field of business, owning and operating various enterprises in greater New York. Colleagues, lay and professional, recently acclaimed him the *ultimate* Garveyite.

A prolific writer, Wilson has penned other pertinent works in education, economics and therapeutic psychology which we hope to share with readers and admirers in the near future.

AWIS Authorized/Authentic AUDIO MP3 CDs by AMOS WILSON

Lecture Titles	CATALOG NUMBER	PRICE
The Third Reconstruction: Moving Beyond Civil and Human Rights into Afrikan Revolution *plus bonus* Who Will Bell the Cat?...	MP911502	$12.00
Who Will Bell the Cat? *De*-constructing the U.S. Violence Initiative	MP921809	$ 7.00
Tools of Empire: Construction, Destruction, and Reconstruction of Afrikan Civilizations 3500BCE to 2100AD	MP199102	$12.00
Black-on-Black Violence: White-engineered Self-annihilation in the Black Community	MP912402	$12.00
Culture and Identity: Critical Analyses and Pragmatic Approaches to Feel-good History and Conspiracy Theories	MP932401	$12.00
European Historiography and Oppression Exposed: An Afrikan Analysis	MP890205	$12.00
Death at an Early Age: The Failure of the American Education System	MP199906	$12.00
Effectuating an Afrikan Revolutionary Psychotherapy	MP840124	$12.00
Afrikan-centered Consciousness, Personality and Culture as Instruments of Power (*misnomered* Blueprint for Black Power)	MP942109	$12.00
European Psychological Warfare Against Afrikans	MP891502	$12.00
The Psychology of Cooperative Economics in the Black Community	MP200006	$12.00
The Crisis of Leadership in the Black Community	MP000000	$12.00
Issues of Manhood in Black and White	MP901125	$12.00
Developing an Afrikan Psychology of Liberation	MP852212	$12.00
Awakening the Natural Genius of Black Children	MP930393	$12.00
Riot or Revolt: The LA Rebellion and Urban Responses to State Injustice and Brutality	MP920601	$12.00
Special Education: Its Special Agenda Unhooded	MP930108	$12.00
The Legacy of Marcus Garvey: The True vs False/Pseudo Nationalist	MP870125	$12.00
The Economic Psychology of Afrikan Nationalism	MP872501	$12.00
The Falsification of Afrikan Consciousness	MP933010	$12.00
Black Male Female Relationships: Searing Perspectives	MP911124	$12.00
Eurocentric Political Dogmatism: Mental Health Mis-Diagnosis of Afrikan People	MP851801	$12.00
Rethinking Education: Star Wars and Millennia Beyond	MP1980XX	$12.00
Black Entertainment White Profits: An Outrage	MP940716	$12.00
The Importance and Challenge of Afrikan Parenting	MP872011	$12.00

Shipping & Handling   1-2 CD Sets $4.95   3-5 CD Sets $6.95   ✳ Call about DVDs
• **Note:** Prices are subject to change without notice. Tel. 718 462-1830